Value for Money Marketing

Value for Money Marketing

A GUIDE TO MEASURING MARKETING PERFORMANCE

RODDY MULLIN

IN ASSOCIATION WITH

Marketing

**KOGAN
PAGE**

First published in 2001

Kogan Page Limited
120 Pentonville Road
London N1 9JN
UK

Kogan Page US
22 Broad Street
Milford CT 06460
USA

British Library Cataloguing in Publication Data

A CIP record for this book is available from the British Library.

ISBN 0 7494 3553 4

Typeset by Jean Cussons Typesetting, Diss, Norfolk
Printed and bound in Great Britain by Biddles Ltd, Guildford and King's Lynn

Contents

Preface

This book is dangerous; it could change your business culture.

It has but one purpose: to persuade you of the benefits of measuring each and every marketing activity so that you can find out whether you are getting value for money from marketing.

Fancy that! Actually knowing that the money you spend on marketing is of value! And being able to show – nay prove even – to all those cynical analysts, shareholders, investors and your own financial staff that you (and they) are truly getting a bang for your buck from each marketing activity.

This is not a dream. You can do it. You can measure marketing activity. This book shows you some mechanisms to use. The solutions are not all-inclusive – rather, they are designed to inspire you to consider measuring the success of marketing activities and then to invent your own approaches or adapt or use the mechanisms given here.

Be persuaded: measure marketing and know that you are getting value from it.

Acknowledgements

To my many volunteer colleagues within the Worshipful Company of Marketors and the Chartered Institute of Marketing, who have become friends and who have helped me to clarify what is important to include in this book. I am grateful to Martin Allen-Perry for providing the gems needed to complete it.

Part 1

Achieving value for money from marketing

Chapter 1 proposes that you should know that you are achieving value for money from marketing. Not knowing should be unacceptable to you. You should implement a value-for-money-from-marketing policy across your whole organization. Everyone responsible for a marketing activity should, at the time they propose that marketing activity, also decide the definition of its success and fund from their budgets a measurement mechanism to allow this success or otherwise to be recorded. In other words, at the same time the marketing activity is proposed its success criteria should be defined. In this book that 'definition of success' or 'success criterion' will be called the 'key performance'. On the completion of the marketing activity its performance is analysed against the key performance indicator and those responsible – for whom work objectives relating to marketing activities have been set – are called to account and praised or otherwise.

Chapter 2 examines, as background information, how marketing activities are arrived at from marketing objectives, themselves derived business objectives, and how marketing itself and the role of the customer fits into a business. Those already familiar with marketing may skip this chapter.

1

Marketing – are you getting value for money?

HOW MARKETING SPENDING SHOULD BE PERCEIVED

When you look back at marketing in your business, over recent weeks or months, you should see a clearly measurable return – that is, substantial evidence of value for money from the amount spent on marketing activities. If you are unsure of what marketing has achieved for you, you need this book. Start today. This book shows you how.

Equally, if you want to know what marketing can achieve for you – especially if you are planning growth or are starting up as a new business – you need to know how successful your marketing is. You need this book too.

Actually, just thinking about measuring achievement is a useful discipline for anyone responsible for a marketing activity. It really makes you think about why you are undertaking any particular marketing activity. Take, for example, advertising in a mature market with just a few players and well-known names of brand and product – think cars here, for instance. If you measure the result of the advertising will it show anything? Probably not. So why do most car advertisements follow the genre and advertise in the same way? It would make more sense to be different, make an impact and increase sales. For example, actually finding out who buys the cars and why and when, then finding more similar persons and targeting them. Then measuring the success of the marketing activity. The key performance indicators would be increased enquiries, increased test drives, increased sales or whatever else has been set as a key performance indicator.

The problem has been the lack of belief that it is actually possible to measure every marketing activity. Some say it has been tried before, but it has never really been tried in a plain straightforward way – where you let the people tasked with the marketing activity define the success criteria and the key performance indicators themselves and then you measure them and prove them right.

The ultimate success criterion is improvement of the bottom line. Do not stray too far from this when setting the definition of success – the key performance indicator – for any marketing activity. 'Customer growth' is not too far from bottom-line improvement, assuming the customers are spenders and buy. In fact you probably need relatively few more of big-spending customers to make an impact and record success. Why not really do your homework and really target the most likely potential big-spending customers? The failure to measure marketing causes frustration for financial directors who see that spend on marketing is often a large – possibly even the largest – part of the budget. They then find it difficult to justify this expenditure in terms of return. This book should remove that frustration.

There is not much advice around to help measure marketing. Return-on-investment-in-marketing packages and packages that measure the relationship between total shareholder return in terms of brand signature are available from top management consultants and analysts. Future packages will allow brand valuations that calculate the bonding strength achieved between brand and customer (essential knowledge for investors – especially as this marketing-based method of analysis is proving better than any other). Guidance for city analysts in London on marketing effectiveness is also being produced in the form of a list of 10 questions to ask of CEOs, with guidance about the analysis of answers. The questions and guidance will be available soon in checklist format from the Worshipful Company of Marketors (WCM).

There are also a few publications available that describe the need to measure value and to make marketing effective or bottom-line accountable (references to a number of them are given in this book). Tim Ambler and Peter Doyle are recent authors of books on the need to measure marketing. Tim Ambler is working with the ICAEW (Institute of Chartered Accountants of England and Wales) to produce a way of measuring brands for the balance sheet. The Chartered Institute of Marketing has started a 'better marketing measurement' campaign in its magazine, *Marketing Business*.

Paul Smith, another author, quotes a source as believing that some 40 per cent of marketing is wasted in terms of return on investment. But one may well ask how does his source know that? People probably suspect it to be true of marketing but who has measured it? Tim Ambler's research on behalf of the Marketing Council found that most firms do not have a clear picture of their overall marketing performance. If you do not know your marketing performance you cannot be measuring marketing, whether as return on investment, bottom line or year-on-year performance.

So what about your firm? Let us assume that your firm is part of the majority that doesn't have a clear picture of their overall marketing performance. How can you become marketing account-able? The solution is twofold:

■ First, the simple but bold expedient of stating that in your orga-nization all marketing activities are to be measured in future.
■ Second, using the necessary measurement mechanisms for which examples upon which you can draw are given in this book.

This book is designed to demonstrate that once you have issued the edict that 'all marketing activity is to be measured in future', your business will not collapse. Yes, it will cost a little more to start with. But once it has operated for a year or two you will know that any money spent on marketing activities will be giving you value for money and, as a bonus, you will have sorted out those persons unable to justify their marketing activities. It really could sharpen up and or get rid of the posers. The obvious need, then, is for measurement mechanisms for marketing activities. For each marketing activity, including those using the new media, this book offers such mechanisms to allow you to know whether you have obtained value for money from marketing.

A mechanism allows you to measure your marketing activities across the board in value terms. You can then compare alternatives in terms of marketing performance. Once a measuring mechanism has been applied to a marketing activity at the budget-setting stage you then can hold those responsible for each marketing activity to account at the end of that activity. Some measurement mechanisms allow continuous monitoring so that, once a marketing activity is under way, you can control and make changes to it.

A controlled marketing operation is quite different from the view of marketing held by some casual observers. Businessmen have been known to consider the marketing department as the equivalent of an incinerator for as much hard-earned cash as they wish to throw at it. In truth, there should be little difference between marketing activity control and the control of all other cash-spending activities. One benefit of measuring marketing activities is that it can lead to control – but not strangulation – of expenditure. Control is achieved by measuring each marketing activity and being able to say, as a result of comparing the outcome with the forecast (the key performance indicator that was set), that each marketing activity was 'value for money'.

Example of measuring marketing activity success in a £64-million-turnover business

In April 2000, at an annual Business Link presentation, Mark Dixon, the managing director of Regus (a fast-growing serviced-office provider) said that he owed his success to marketing. (A rare and brave man in those days!)

He had had the foresight, at the start of 1999, to measure the awareness of businessmen of the concept of the serviced office. Only 7 per cent of businessmen surveyed were aware of the concept at the time. At the end of the year he measured it again and found that it had grown to 54 per cent. This was used to demonstrate to his board and shareholders that the money spent on the marketing objective 'to improve awareness' had worked. This claim was supported by the bottom line, which showed that he had made a profit, and by managers of his serviced offices reporting near 100 per cent occupancy.

So he had three ways to measure value and success in meeting one of the marketing objectives, which he could use in his report to shareholders and the board. This is all that we advocate – measure marketing activity. Prove to yourself and others that your marketing activities are giving you a reasonable return.

Example – marketing activity failure to date in a small business

In November 2000, Simon, a hairdresser – the owner of Snips of Fulham – found that all of his advertising for three months in the local paper had not brought him a customer. How did he know? He had asked everyone who came for a haircut. So no 'value for money' from this marketing activity for Simon.

He is now going to try with a poster on each platform of Fulham Broadway Underground station on the advice of his customers. He spent a couple of hours on the platform watching people. Will this poster succeed? Who knows – but he will certainly be measuring the feedback as before. So he has grasped the principle that we advocate in this book – that of measuring each marketing activity. In fact Simon is having second thoughts about the poster site now; the staff quite often unwittingly hide it behind moveable noticeboards. Fulham Broadway station is also undergoing repair.

He has, of course, chosen to approach marketing using a trial-and-error process. He is not going to ask a professional marketer what he should do. He believes that asking a professional marketer would be expensive. Not that he has bothered to find out if that is true – nor is he aware he could have sought value for money from an appropriate fixed-price deal (see later in this book) with a professional marketer with expertise in the marketing of personal services such as haircutting.

However the professional marketer would certainly have saved the three months of local paper advertising for Simon – when on many days he and his assistant were idle. By chance, the author's own company has helped another client to research haircutting. We know from that research that local papers are not the media channel used by people to seek somewhere for a haircut.

So what else might Simon do? Approaching the personnel managers of local firms is perhaps a better route. Perhaps Simon should offer, through personnel managers of participating firms, a special incentive of a cut-price haircut voucher to be included with pay slips. But in this day and age why not offer something quite different – prepayment Internet booking of haircuts? Simon would need a merchant to take credit card transactions. He would need to develop a Web site and the back room/front room links. But he would certainly be quite different from his competitors for a time – that is until they catch up with him. But by then he would have a customer base loyal to his salon – assuming that his haircuts remain excellent.

He could, of course, later sell copies of his Web site format and the booking software to haircutting businesses three miles away or more, expanding his original business. Why three miles? Yes – how far people are prepared to travel for a haircut has been researched. It depends on the modes of transport available, whether the potential customers are based in rural or urban areas and, of course, a few other factors apply.

CONTROL AND MEASUREMENT APPLIED TO MARKETING ACTIVITY

Why measure marketing?

There are not many books on marketing that deal with the measurement of marketing. A number refer to measurement but from a different perspective than is taken in this book. Look first at why marketing should be measured. Tim Ambler states that marketing should be measured because:

■ marketing secures financial objectives;
■ marketing discourages short termism;
■ marketers (*anyone responsible for a marketing activity*) should be accountable;

■ market-orientated, customer-focused companies are more profitable;
■ market measurement is essential for debriefing.

The author of this book agrees with these reasons.

Tim Ambler's research finds that most firms do not have an idea of their marketing performance. The research showed that firms most commonly measure the following:

■ awareness;
■ market share;
■ relative price;
■ number of complaints;
■ consumer satisfaction;
■ distribution/sustainability;
■ total number of customers;
■ perceived quality/esteem;
■ loyalty/retention;
■ relative perceived quality.

Tim Ambler advocates measuring:

■ sales;
■ marketing investment;
■ bottom-line profit;
■ relative satisfaction with brands;
■ commitment to brands (both from customers and employees);
■ relative perceived quality;
■ relative price;
■ availability;
■ awareness and commitment to goals (both strategic and for employees);
■ active innovation support at the strategic level and number of innovations learnt;
■ adequate resource provision for strategy;
■ appetite for learning and freedom to fail (culture and for employees);
■ the percentage of revenue from launches in the last three years.

These are all admirable measures but are far less easy to implement than what is being proposed here.

The approach here is to say that you should measure *everything*. Then you will see if you have found value for money and that your marketing is effective. This is the difference in this book's approach from every other book. This book is trying to convince you to measure everything just like an accountant. Imagine an accountant not measuring every penny!

Measuring marketing activity is practical and the mechanisms for measurement that are suggested here are simple to put in place. The suggestions made here are illustrative – they are measurement mechanisms that you might use or adapt. The mechanisms will also highlight where your firm is not being well served – where you are being taken for a ride. The principle of insisting on measuring applies to any form of marketing activity. Even using marketing consultants. Here Tim Ambler agrees, for he suggests that marketing specialists should be measured against the value they add.

He urges setting up a board-level task force to assess the marketing metrics to use in a firm. Marketing metrics measure a firm's marketing performance but not necessarily every marketing activity. This is a top-down approach. In the view of the author of this book, setting up a task force is a potential recipe for loss of focus and certainly one with prevarication potential. (Isn't that what committees do?) This book adopts a different approach that involves most people with responsibility; all that has to be done is to tell everyone that every marketing activity has to be measured. It will more readily produce results than a task force and will do it much sooner.

Tim Ambler, despite being a chartered accountant, fights shy of insisting that your accountant should oversee the measurement. He does mention it. He mentions it in an earlier book too; but why not insist on your accountant doing the measuring? Your accountant is good at measuring and if you are a small business others will be busy or inexperienced at measuring. Leave the responsibility for deciding what to measure to the person responsible for the marketing activity, but give the actual counting and analysis to someone else, say your accountant. You may have to train your accountant. S/he could even enjoy it. Accountants have always wanted to get their hands on marketing so it should not be difficult to persuade yours to carry out the measuring marketing activity for someone else in your team. Others accept that accountants measure their spending of money and compare it with their budget. Just add measuring the marketing activity mechanism to their jobs.

Peter Doyle brilliantly describes marketing's lost influence in the UK and the need to restore it, with marketing shareholder value as the solution. He strongly supports the contention that the only strategy for survival and profitable return is that of maximizing shareholder value. He sees no conflict between marketing and shareholder value. He recognizes that marketing has not been integrated with financial value creation, yet 'marketing-led growth is at the heart of value creation'. He puts into perspective the full effect of the new information age/electronic environment. He describes intranets, extranets and disintermediation well, and the potential they have to improve on 'downstream' activity, cutting out all middlemen and producing improved customer communication while 'upstream' closer co-operation with suppliers – a virtual organization – reduces assets required to support rapid growth and maximizes flexibility. He does not add how much easier it is in this age to measure marketing activity. His book has a focus that to attract outside funds the return on investment has to be greater than the cost of capital, that is maximising shareholder value – where the market value exceeds the book value. He believes marketers need to focus on creating shareholder value.

Peter Doyle states that 'marketing expenditures like any other can be wasted and satisfied customers are not necessarily profitable ones' and offers a solution to overcome this problem.

Even if satisfied customers are not profitable ones, hopefully they refer and recommend. Doyle differentiates between conventional approaches to budgeting and value-based budgeting. This book's measurement mechanisms should allow you to adopt either approach and move to a value-based approach if you accept his proposition.

He recognizes the need to distinguish between low- and high-involvement marketing communications, reflecting the difference between an established business and a new business.

The approach of this book to measurement is to use many common yardsticks – measurements that you probably use now, such as measuring sales of each product and service split by customer, by area and by type of customer. The book suggests other ways of measuring that you may not have considered.

Three points to make it easier to implement a 'measuring marketing activity' culture

Point one – measure all marketing activity

Tell everyone that every marketing activity has to be measured. Giving out such an instruction is easy. Your instruction to the whole firm simply states:

> All marketing activity is to be measured in future. The person responsible for each marketing activity is in future also responsible for deciding the success measure – the key performance indicator – and the measurement mechanism to prove that the marketing activity is value for money and including the cost of that measurement in their budget costs. The start date is to be…

(See below for how to decide the best start date.)

This statement or edict should be both a challenge and one small step towards a culture change.

This book describes plenty of alternative mechanisms for measuring marketing activity.

At the end of the day, when the person responsible is called to account, whatever has been measured should be the justification for saying that he or she has done a good job, proving the marketing activity to have value for money. Choosing an appropriate mechanism will also allow interim monitoring and allow changes to be introduced while the marketing activity is under way. This interim monitoring can be as fast as you wish – even in real time. More of this later.

Point two – keep everything simple

Keep everything simple – the marketing activity budget setting, the selection of the key performance indicator, the implementation of the marketing activity, the measurement and the feedback process. It is not difficult, then, to control marketing activity.

This book gives examples of how to do this later on.

Point three – define clearly the boundary for each marketing activity

The third point is that it is much easier to measure a marketing activity if one person only is responsible for it. You must not split a marketing activity. For example you should not allow several people to produce literature to promote a brand – even if you have heavily policed guidelines to ensure consistency. In practice guidelines alone often do not work. Better still, make only one person responsible for a brand and every activity that stems from it. Then you can measure success.

When then do you start to implement the instruction for everyone to measure marketing?

Start from any time in the year. Let people try out mechanisms for measuring marketing means before your start date by all means. Let people put in a bit of practice. But fix a start date some time ahead. A good idea is to start from the beginning of the accounting year, say, or from the start of your appraisal year when you set work objectives. The measurement of marketing activity occurs alongside budget setting, when you consider the cost of each marketing activity – when you give out targets or set work objectives. That is the time to define success and declare the key performance indicator and its metric.

Do not be surprised that this book includes measuring marketing achievement by individuals. Measure everything that is a marketing activity. Sales is a part of marketing and firms have been measuring sales persons' performance for years. This book just extends the person measurement that is now happening in sales to all others involved in marketing. Such a proposal should cheer up your hard-done-by sales force. They will love it.

The logical point of the formal process of setting mechanisms to measure marketing activity is to start and work alongside the setting of the marketing objectives. Marketing objectives come from business objectives. Business objectives arise from carrying out a business audit and a business objectives setting process. This can be both simple and straightforward if you wish. Larger firms formalize and sometimes complicate the process. An example follows at the end of this section on setting business objectives and in Chapter 2 an actual example is included. Look at those examples now if you are uncertain how to arrive at business objectives.

How do you set about measuring all marketing activity?

The marketing objectives, marketing activities, definitions of success (the key performance indicator), measurement of marketing activities and budget-setting process all follow from the business objective setting process. This process includes:

▪ *Marketing objectives/marketing activities/budgets:* A process where marketing objectives are constructed from the business objectives and marketing activities are then defined to achieve each marketing objective. Not surprisingly every part of each marketing activity is costed, following a standard process. This is where clear boundaries of responsibility come in – activities must be grouped together within one cost centre, including staff, overheads and so forth. This probably happens within any firm – it is just that a marketing activity must not be spread across two spending cost centres. So far so good but do not stop there – you now need to set the mechanism of measurement for each marketing activity.

▪ *Deciding and setting 'measurement of achievement' – mechanisms for marketing activities:* This is probably new to most organizations. Each marketing activity is examined and its successful achievement is forecast – that is, it is given a key performance indicator and a mechanism is found to measure that achievement. Sometimes you need to measure the same thing before the activity starts in order to make comparison with how well the activity has done at the end (see the example of Regus above). This book provides examples of measurement mechanisms for a wide range of marketing activities. It is for you to decide what is success – the key performance indicator – and the metric or mechanism you are going to use to measure it. Be inventive. Be creative. But do it. For each marketing activity you then decide and include the cost of the mechanism with which you are going to measure it. This may form one or more additional marketing-sponsored activities entered within the costing for the marketing activity. You must insist that a different person is to carry out the measurement part or at least the analysis of it. That person should be your accountant.

▪ *Marketing measurement activity – feedback at the end*: The results of the measurement, when compared with your key performance indicator, confirm the achievement of your marketing activity – or tells you that you did not achieve it.

■ *Marketing control – both ongoing and at the end*: If you want to be able to assess progress during a marketing activity then you need to use a mechanism that allows you to measure ongoing achievement. This allows correcting activity to be made – for example measuring response to TV advertising in real time may suggest that one advertisement is better than another, which offers the opportunity to switch to more frequent use of the more responsive advertisement.

Then at the end of the marketing activity you hold your version of 'calling people to account' for value for money. (This book does not propose to suggest how you carry this out. The third degree, summary execution or praise, a holiday with all expenses paid. We can all fantasize.)

Some typical mechanisms for measuring marketing activity

By way of example, measuring marketing activities can be carried out through feedback using mechanisms to measure in terms of any or a combination of the following:

■ orders taken, sales made;
■ the source of sales or orders;
■ call centre reports;
■ a market research survey of a percentage of the target market demonstrating awareness;
■ a questionnaire/registration that allows you to confirm you have a particular type of potential customer;
■ a Web site visitor count, or web site tracking;
■ a supplier assurance (though these may not always be truthful – as you will see).

The marketing measurement mechanism feedback closes the loop, just as bookkeepers' books account for cash spend under different headings that closes the 'where the money has been spent' loop.

An example of a simple business process: from business objectives to marketing activities

The business process may be as simple as a rational discussion among board members arising from a study of the resources available that concludes that 'the business has the resources and the will to grow by 10 per cent in size and – assuming there is no problem to that size of growth in the market – we want to achieve the same percentage profit overall.' In large businesses the process is more complex, but generally you need both the resources and the will to tackle each business objective.

Assuming you are able to confirm that there are no market forces of a size or importance that would hinder growth (this is where the marketer is drawn into the business audit and business setting process for advice – see the London solicitors' firms example below) then, from the statement above, the following business objectives might result: 'We want the business to grow by 10 per cent' and 'we want to achieve the same percentage profit overall'.

The marketing objectives, then, might include all or some of the following, that:

■ we are to increase orders from existing customers and this is to account for 5 per cent of growth;
■ we will do this by offering them new replacement products/services, as well as persuading them to buy more existing products/services;
■ we are to find new customers for both new and existing products/services ranges, say 4 per cent; and
■ (more rarely) we are to take new products/services to new customers, the last 1 per cent in this case.

The marketing activities for the old customers may include direct mail, e-mails, sales visits, incentives and, to reduce the cost of ordering, persuasion to use the Web site for ordering – so reducing the cost of order processing and retention of, or improving on, the existing profit margin.

The marketing activities for new customers may include some PR, some advertising including a Web site to create awareness and educate the new customers and so on...

As each marketing activity is proposed then it needs to be checked that it fits within a single person's responsibility, costed according to your normal methods and then the key performance indicator and measurement mechanism for feedback should be set. For example, mechanisms might include:

■ supplying each direct mailshot with an order form with a unique code to monitor the return (which is persuading, as your key performance indicator, 90 per cent of existing customers to order 10 per cent more at 5 per cent discount if they change over to Web site ordering);

■ using a different code if customers enter and order from the Web site directly rather than by telephone or by mail – at the end of the year compare the actual results to see if 90 per cent did order 10 per cent more through the Web;

■ measuring registrations as an indication of doing more than just 'entering the shop' – for each incentive or Web site offer use a different home page on which to enter the site and register;

■ for an advertisement, asking customers responding to quote a unique code; if response is to a Web site then hits give an indication of advertisement success (but not of the site itself – that is measured in other ways); the same coding can be collected at a call centre;

■ training your sales staff to ask for the trigger. Did the customer see an advertisement? In which paper? Perhaps they heard about it from someone – who? This way, unsolicited orders may suggest a future marketing activity. Recording if a customer saw an advertisement and where is a measurement mechanism.

During the marketing activity your appointed measurer collects and collates the replies. Finally the measurer compares the achieved results with the forecast of achievement. Value for money?

Assuming your forecast was realistic, the result if equal or better will then demonstrate you have received value for money.

If it has not then you should be better equipped to understand why not for next time.

A marketer should be able to recommend and then deliver each marketing activity with the key performance indicator and the metric or mechanism to measure achievement defined and thus prove the achievement as being value for money.

WHO IS THE MARKETER?

A marketer is anyone in the company who you are using to achieve your marketing objectives and who is spending your money on any marketing activity. Marketers are responsible for marketing activities. In the CRM/eCRM/e-commerce environment there are more, rather than fewer, people involved. It is possible that everyone may be involved. If you achieve this you probably have a firm that is fully customer focused – well done.

The marketer can be external, for example any one person or different persons or a team from any of the following:

■ advertising agency;
■ public relations agency;
■ exhibition design team;
■ call centre;
■ market research agency;
■ a Webmaster.

The external person may be supported by creative or design staff.

The marketer can be internal and might include people at either director or manager level (we use manager here):

■ the IT manager responsible for a CRM (customer relationship management) programme;
■ your sales manager;
■ your service department – customer manager, complaints manager, key account managers;
■ your marketing staff – advertising manager, PR manager, marketing communications manager;
■ your in-house call centre manager;
■ a regional office manager with a delegated but single responsibility for a marketing activity.

Marketers reading the paragraphs above may feel that this is unfair, especially as they have been trained in marketing and this book seems to be advocating a whole range of persons as marketers. What we are not recommending is that you should use any of the above persons if they are not trained.

The Chartered Institute of Marketing (CIM) runs many courses designed to train anybody from any discipline in the appropriate part of marketing for the task in hand. Find them on the CIM Web site: www.cim.co.uk, or call (+44) (0)1628 427200 for CIM training.

CAN THIS BOOK HELP YOU OBTAIN VALUE FOR MONEY FROM MARKETING?

This book is structured to consider all the aspects of marketing that you are likely to face, whether you are a small or medium enterprise, or a large corporation. The principles do not change even if your business has only a single person carrying out everything, or a series of departments all reporting into a marketing director.

Clearly, a degree of sophistication is required for the larger business, and a section is included for what are described as advanced techniques. This is contributed by Professor Robert Shaw of Cranfield – an expert on marketing metrics. Do not be deterred – the principles that are given in this section will work for the smaller business too. What attracted the author to ask Robert Shaw? His no-nonsense hard-hitting introduction to his book *Improving Marketing Effectiveness* (The Economist Books, 1998). He was one of the first to advocate the need to measure marketing activity. His contribution is of updated extracts from Part 2, Chapter 7 and all the tools of Part 3 of his book along with an extract of an article published in *Marketing Business* in March 2001.

This book is written for the marketer as an aide memoire, for the managing director who wants to know whether he or she is getting maximum value for money from marketing. It is also for other professionals in the business who need an insight into what the marketing hype is about, and how it can be controlled – financial directors especially. It is also for the advanced student. Measuring marketing is not yet set at diploma level or below.

Remember, in marketing you need flair, the ability to create something different that really captures the imagination. You need the ability to convert a product of which the customer – the public – is unaware into something that sells like hot cakes. A marketer should also be able to measure the success of marketing activities and for each one define its contribution (to the Tim Ambler bottom line or the Peter Doyle shareholder value) and how that compares with the success expected when the activity was first decided and its mechanism to measure achievement. Remember that the fear of failure or actually recording one activity as a failure should not mean cutting marketing back to the bone, for this may mean that only the mundane can be carried out. This could well lead to failure to achieve any marketing objective whatever. A failed marketing activity should present the opportunity to try something else. But at least you will have been able to measure the extent of the failure and you will be able to compare it with alternative marketing activities that you then employ – like Simon at Snips of Fulham.

Equally important, using a mechanism to measure achievement of marketing activity gives feedback and allows you to recognize where you may be taken for a ride – being overcharged or sold something with more bells and whistles than can be justified. Included in these pages are management failures in suppliers or scams to watch out for, some practised by well-known names.

This text is designed to allow anyone to question how each marketing activity forms an element of marketing that can be attributed to an objective. It allows scope to assess suppliers – the external marketers you may be employing. Worry if any supplier is unhappy to have a key performance indicator and metric set for marketing measurement for the activity for which you are paying.

Cautionary tale – measure the activity of your supplier too

A client, despite being advised not to do so, succumbed to the temptation to use advertising by fax.

He agreed to pay a large sum after being persuaded that he would achieve a substantial return from the 12,000 faxes that would be sent out.

In the end he received not a single enquiry, so he refused to pay. The judge in the Dorset court ruled that as an experienced businessman he should have known better – so he had to pay.

To this day he does not know if a single fax was even sent, let alone whether it was the message that was wrong or the fax address list or that any faxes were received.

So what could he have done? Here are a few ideas:

■ he might have insisted in the contract on a certain minimum return level;
■ he might have insisted on being given say 120 names (1 per cent) on which he could check on physical receipt, and on understanding and acceptance of the message;
■ he should have insisted on a test of, say, 120 names at the start and only if a percentage response was achieved would he have proceeded with the whole contract.

The advertising fax company is still in business.

How to make financial and budgeting more difficult for marketing

Budgeting and controlling marketing spending can be made really difficult if the structure and organization of your business allows many people access to amounts of money to spend on marketing. If each director, say, has access to promotional cash not set against any objective, then do not be surprised if it achieves nothing at all or it is counterproductive. If you have marketing and sales activities in different parts of the business you create further problems – unless you have very clear, complementary objectives with no overlap. Even this rarely works. The same may apply if you have merchandising and sales staff reporting to different managers ('North' and 'South', say) and a third manager centrally responsible for marketing – all reporting to different directors. 'Sales' is a part of 'marketing', alongside every other part of marketing, whether public relations, new product development or any marketing communications activity. The need to creat clear responsibilities is apparent. If you are trying to develop a corporate brand you will fail if you let everyone spend money on promotion; you could find several designs of your firm's logo on clothing existing if they are not cleared, controlled centrally – or, better still, one person's responsibility.

Sometimes it is necessary to give other people marketing money for one-off tasks. Here separating and making clear the responsibility for the marketing activity is important. For example, if it is to support a number of regional marketing promotions (a marketing objective) yet you wish to have a consistent corporate brand (another one of your marketing objectives). Just letting the various regions do the lot themselves will not necessarily make it easy to measure or actually achieve either objective. So make the provision of T-shirts (the corporate branding bit) one person's responsibility and measure the effectiveness of the T-shirts (and other corporate items). Make the regional promotional event marketing activity the responsibility of another person probably from the region but also with measurement activity. Think through the consequence of marketing activities.

Untrained, unskilled marketers

Sadly, marketers are not perfect. Some are untrained, and may be skilled at hiding their limitations. Some are not keeping up to date with the needs of the profession.

A survey in 2000 found that 250,000 people in London had the word marketing in their job title. Of these only 4,000 belonged to the Chartered Institute of Marketing in Central London. Would you employ an unqualified non-professional accountant? Why not employ a chartered marketer? They exist (about 3,500 of them in January 2001) and they are growing in numbers.

A few marketers believe that accountability should not be part of their remit – I hope they will not be around for much longer. I also hope that your firm is not employing them at present.

The rip-off factor

There are also a number of scams around and 'management weaknesses' in suppliers of the marketing communications services that are your marketing activities. This book covers some of the ones of which you should be aware and describes ways to expose them.

Only the facts are given – you are left to draw your own conclusions.

LIMITATIONS OF THIS BOOK

This book does not cover specific marketing techniques, such as how to produce advertisements, check printers' proofs or task a PR agency. These are described in companion books in the Kogan Page range, especially the Marketing in Action Series. This book is about how to be in control of marketing and obtain value through measuring marketing activity. It complements the other books in the series. To help you it makes reference to other books and also provides a list by topic in an appendix.

This book does not cover marketing metrics leading to market valuation or indeed to a brand evaluation. The approach to these topics is covered elsewhere. References are given to these other texts.

In order to exercise control, you need to measure in an appropriate way, you need to be aware of scams or just plain poor performance of a marketing activity in-house or by suppliers and this then allows you to budget more accurately and hence justify, in financial terms, your spend on marketing. To an extent this book will allow both the efficiency and effectiveness of marketing to be found. Marketing metrics alone gives just an indication of effectiveness.

A useful, quick and practical book on marketing is *How to be Better at Marketing* by Rod Davey and Anthony Jacks, which is a practical volume, and Patrick Forsyth has produced a valuable book, *Marketing on a Tight Budget*, which is also practical and gives inexpensive ideas for marketing (both Kogan Page, 2000). And in *Great Answers to Tough Marketing Questions* (Kogan Page, 1999) Paul Smith has produced the written equivalent of a Web site's 'frequently asked questions', which takes the mystery out of marketing and also features an exciting format – read it cover-to-cover or dip in. He gives answers to 114 questions such as:

■ Why are most companies weak at marketing? (Ninety per cent of British companies do not know their customers.)
■ How do you develop a positioning? (Lucozade is an example –

it was changed from a drink for the sick to a drink for sports people.)

■ What are the mental stages of making a purchase?

■ Why don't great products win all the time? (No one knows about them, they are wrongly positioned, they are not available when people want them or they are too expensive.)

■ If a product retails at £9.99, what price can a manufacturer charge? (About £4!)

2

The marketing process

This chapter describes how marketing fits into a business. It is included here so that everyone starts from the same standpoint. Please feel that you can skip this chapter if you are already a marketer – or just skim it if you want to see how the book looks at marketing within a business. The reason the chapter is included is because if marketing is to be made easy, in order to meet the need to create single responsibility for marketing activities within a business, and then to define success (the key performance indicator and its metric) and then measure that to find out if you have succeeded and obtained value for money marketing, that can only be achieved by first describing how marketing fits into a business.

FITTING MARKETING INTO THE BUSINESS

Any organization is likely to have some vision for the long term and from that some objectives for the immediate future will arise. The business objectives do not need to be ambitious – they do not need to be set down, although it helps. When they are set down it is called a business plan.

From these business objectives, marketing objectives arise. For example, if you want to grow the business by 10 per cent then that becomes a target. It can be quantified as a marketing objective – if you have 400 customers, 10 per cent growth is 40 more. You also know that the extra customers to achieve that growth will not just appear: you have to go and get them in. Further you know that not everyone who you approach will buy, so you will need to tell a lot more, just to be sure of finding 40 – but how many more? There are plenty of other questions. How do they decide to buy things and in particular from your business? How are you going to tell them about what you have for sale? Such questions begin to help formulate other marketing objectives than the straightforward first marketing objective of finding 40 more customers.

Which marketing activities you select to achieve your marketing objectives will in large part be decided by your customers – which is why this chapter explores the customer. For example, you may speculate that if all your customers watch commercial television then you should advertise there; but if none of your customers watch commercial television then it is not worth advertising there. Common sense tells you that; but there are much more subtle differences, such as the times they watch, the programmes, etc. Through what media you should communicate with your potential customers becomes important. Thinking from a customer viewpoint will point you towards implementing marketing activities to resolve marketing objectives. But you have to research that viewpoint first.

The chapter looks at marketing activities that can be fitted into the business process to find out about customers. This is simply to help you decide business objectives. Marketing activities are generally available to support the non-operational side of the business but are often less used. The operational parts of the business are more obvious and the marketing activities are described here too.

There is a difference between how marketing in an established business is tackled and how marketing is approached in a new business. In an established business you have customers – these customers can be very helpful in fine-tuning your business to meet their needs. But when starting a business you do not have any customers and so you need a high level of research and promotional marketing activities.

In an established market, there is still a need to sustain awareness and educate but to a lesser extent. You will probably need to do it in a subtle way. Innovation comes into its own to make purchase exciting as a product or service matures. In an established business your clients will often tell you where you have gone wrong. Professor John Quelch, Dean of London Business School, in his address to Lexcel achievers at the Law Society in October 2000, stressed the importance of listening to complaints. Research shows, he said, that most complainers are trying to help you improve your business.

A lot more effort needs to be put into creating awareness and educating the potential buyers of the services or products you are offering when they are new to the customer and you are a new business. You do not have a client database from which to readily get feedback. If you want feedback you will probably have to both arrange for it and pay for it.

The basic business process applied to arrive at marketing objectives is the same in each case. This chapter continues by examining the common elements.

Business audit and planning process

The business process of analysis is usually carried out annually, often based on statutory timings. A number of organizations now carry out the activity at six-monthly intervals; this maintains a pressure on management that is considered to be beneficial.

The direction in which a business is going needs to be determined at the start of the process and is described as the *vision*. When times are hard, or the owners or board are unambitious, the vision may be one of mere survival. At another extreme it may be to become global market leader. This is not impossible. For example, take a firm in Peckham, London, that makes petroleum hoses. It is one of only six firms in the world making such hoses. So it could become a global leader if it wished to do so and selected such a vision. A vision may equally be a simple one – say, to achieve a percentage growth improvement on the previous year or stay as you are. Having a vision is helpful.

Without a vision a business will drift. The vision should be ong term, with a number of interim goals. The vision will determine how much resource is devoted to such activities as operations, marketing, research and development. The vision should encompass the shareholder need for growth in shareholder value.

Once a vision is agreed it is helpful to set a *focus*. People work better with it. When they have a clear focus, staff can respond more

Table 2.1 Example – professional services partnership business plan

	Partners' objectives	Group objectives	Key work objectives
Financial	£**m turnover with current staff numbers and costs and at least a 1.06 multiplier or 5% profit margin when considered as a company. Plus growth of eight additional fee earners with no extra support to give four active groups (15% in total numbers equals 25% increase in fee earners).	Achieve or improve on the target multipliers for the group projects in the anticipated final fees and costs.	Achieve or improve on the target multipliers for the projects in the anticipated final fees and costs in which an individual is employed.
Operations	Maintain sufficient technical, management, accommodation and administration support for 1 above. Performance to meet or exceed function, time and cost.	Performance to meet or exceed function, time and cost for 1 above.	Performance to meet or exceed function, time and cost for 1 above. Takes responsibility for own technical design, ensures project programmes are agreed, monitored and met, ensures resource planning and control are agreed, monitored and met, ensures QA sign off information, etc, is actioned. Where hold specialist technical skill: lead the firm in agreed topics. Undertake defined group administrative tasks.
Marketing	Market firm to achieve workload for 1 above. Partners to develop and maintain PR and awareness activities as a contribution to prestige of firm or which results in opportunities for work.	Group to maintain, encourage and develop links with past and potential clients/customers which leads to opportunities for work. Encourage individuals to develop and maintain PR and awareness activities as a	To maintain, encourage and develop individual links with past and potential clients/customers. The measure is by recording marketing non-productive time that leads to opportunities for firm to obtain work. Individuals to develop and maintain PR and awareness

Table 2.1 (continued)

		contribution to prestige of firm.	activities as a contribution to prestige of firm.
Customer care	Keep clients/customers happy. The measure is no major complaints as ascertained by partners on routine calls to clients and by independent client review.	Keep clients/customers happy. The measure is no major complaints as ascertained by partners on routine calls to clients and by independent client review.	Keep clients/customers happy. The measure is no major complaints as ascertained by partners on routine calls to clients and by independent client review.
Employee care	Keep staff happy. Maintain/improve retention rate. Develop subordinates through training for promotion or specialists posts.	Keep staff happy. Maintain/improve retention rate. Develop subordinates through training for promotion or for specialist posts.	Keep staff happy. Behaviour, attitude, team building; play full part as defined. If a supervisor or any other staff maintain/improve retention rate and develop subordinates through training, for promotion or for specialists posts.
Retain professional	Maintain, encourage and measure individual; 50 hours continuing professional development programme per year.	Maintain, encourage and measure individual; 50 hours continuing professional development programme per year.	Undertake individual 50 hours continuing professional development programme per year.
Partner well-being	Keep ourselves as partners happy – by achieving above objectives at an average of 50 hours per week worked and through delegation, with no significant health problems.		

readily to situations or to difficulties when trouble arises. A focus is usually short term and can be seen as a step towards the vision.

When a Connex rail passenger arrived at Waterloo in a train that had been so delayed that there was no chance of her reaching Edinburgh that night, the manager found her a taxi to take her there. This was marvellous publicity for the company and merited an entry in the Guinness Book of Records for the largest taxi fare ever paid. The Connex focus at that time ('getting passengers there') was clearly understood.

A focus should be carefully crafted to encompass what the business is about to achieve – the short-term vision.

From vision and focus, a number of objectives can be set. The objectives are measurable and have a time deadline.

A useful way to see if any objective will work is to test it against the SMART criteria. The letters stand for:

S = Specific
M = Measurable
A = Agreed
R = Reasonable
T = Timebound

What it means is that an objective should not be vague. 'Specific' implies a figure, a target, with the 'timebound' giving a date when the objective should be achieved. 'Measurable' means just that. 'Agreed' is giving an objective that all those involved agree with. 'Reasonable' is probably more difficult because often there is an external environmental dimension.

Before the objectives are publicized it is worth carrying out a check to see if the SMART criteria – particularly the R = Reasonable – applies across the market as well as just for your firm. The market capacity must be there for the objectives to be achievable.

Here is an example of the need for market confirmation. At a professional services marketing conference in 1997, specially commissioned research found that each firm of solicitors with representatives attending the conference had a growth objective for the year of between 3 per cent and 8 per cent.

However for the market as a whole there was no growth in legal business forecast for that year.

Therefore, the only way any growth could be achieved was at

the expense of other firms. No firm had plans to attack and knock out the competition. Their objectives were not SMART in a total market sense.

Once the business objectives are set, a business plan is in effect and from this a budget can be drawn up. Some firms set this whole process down on paper as a business plan. Producing a written business plan is a sensible way of communicating what you are trying to achieve. It is useful because it allows others to obtain a picture of your business. It is also useful if you are able to add the reasoning behind the decisions – it is really helpful when you look back next year and in future years.

A business plan should not be long – never more than about 20 pages including financial tables. Financial tables are often best produced in graphical form; many people who are not 'figures minded' prefer this form of display. The financial part of a business plan allocates resource in cash terms to each objective. Some of these cash resources are for marketing – make sure that sufficient cash is allocated for marketing activities.

Table 2.1 is an example in table format of a professional services firm business plan – just the objectives part. The example business plan is constructed starting with partner objectives. It is then broken down into the objectives that stem from that.

The work objectives for individuals are used to help achievement of their Investors in People-based appraisal system. Note how the individuals have marketing 'work' objectives themselves. Note too how marketing fits into the business objectives. It is now possible to take the marketing objectives given in the table and split them up into marketing activities.

Each of the marketing activities is then considered and the criteria for achievement are defined. The key performance indicator and its metric – a mechanism or mechanisms for measurement of that achievement criterion – are decided. Finally it is decided who is to measure and analyse the results. Everything, all marketing activities and mechanisms, is costed. All the costs are fed into the budget.

STARTING WITH THE CUSTOMER

This part of the chapter describes what marketing can do for you to improve your understanding of the customer and their understanding of you.

Why do you need to start with the customer?

The days of customers buying what they are offered are gone. The customer has an amazing amount of choice. Customers are affected by their background, their social or cultural influences, they consider and think of matters in different ways, they have varied economic purchasing power, their intelligence varies, they have prejudices.

Clearly you need to understand your customers whether they are existing customers or potential customers. You need to find out all about them to serve them better, retain their custom and persuade them to buy more. Everyone in your organization needs to know about them. Equally, the customers will be finding out about your company. It is two-way communication in which you will establish a relationship. Making sure you do that well and that the customer trusts your firm is called 'customer relationship management'. You should aim 'to provide a consistent customer experience wherever the customer touches you each time' (this is the Abbey National's aim – an excellent one; note the use of the word 'consistent' – one of the 'six Cs' – see later in this chapter).

Next you need to create a favourable and appropriate perception and image about your company and its products/services – ideally so that customers think that their perception of your firms product/service provides the answer when a need arises at the moment that need occurs in their mind. The development of ownership of a part of a person's mind is called 'brand creation'. Fixing that brand deeply is called 'brand bonding'. When a person buys only your brand you have ultimate success. This is being achieved by clever marketing.

You need to understand how customers buy and establish a sales process that matches their buying process.

You need to know how those around the customer can influence their buying behaviour.

Why is it important to start with the customer in marketing? The following parts to this question are identified:

■ It is of key importance to think from the customer viewpoint – many firms and even marketers do not do this.

■ The effect of branding on the customer is very powerful if the branding is properly done.

■ Selling to the customer should involve an understanding of the buying process adopted by the customer and should involve the development of a sales process to match.

■ In this computer age it is possible to use knowledge management to help sales understand the customer and the customer view.

■ Customers are influenced by others when making purchases and this influence must be understood.

Example of failing to start with the customer

A firm of marketing consultants was called by a client to examine why, despite high turnover, they were making a loss selling leather jackets at 43 concession outlets in department stores across UK.

The consultants found that the client had stocked the concessions (and continued to stock them) with products that took no account of the customer needs. In the north of UK they had assumed people would buy jackets with arms and in the south without. They were wrong. The customers in the south buy jackets with arms and in the north they buy them without. They are tough up north. In the south they want a full jacket – value for money.

So how did they lose money? They had a policy of supplying a customer within 24 hours with the jacket they wanted if it was available in any of their other stores. It usually was. So the staff spent all the time (and profit) telephoning, moving jackets to and fro, all by special delivery. Had they asked the customer beforehand – applying a very small amount of market research – they would have made some profit on their £1 million turnover.

Marketing starts with the customer

Identifying your customer and establishing a customer profile – an idealized, averaged, but complete understanding of the way that customers think, influenced by how, when, what, and from whom they are prepared to buy – is really important: without customers you make no sales. With no sales a business dies. Marketing is tasked with identifying and knowing the customer. If you discover that there is more than one common type of customer the different but identifiable separate customer groups are known as segments. Sorting all types of customers by segments is called market segmentation. Market segmentation is only helpful where each segment has a size, purchasing power, accessibility, future viability from which to make a profit.

If you are selling to buyers and the buyers are selling on your product or service to consumers, marketing will need to understand both tiers of customers – that is, the primary buyers and the primary buyers' own buyers. If you are dealing with business-to-business customers, their customers too may be business customers. There are differences within each tier.

A client makes and supplies products for the retail gift trade and sells them to several kinds of shops. These range from department stores to craft outlets and seaside gift shops. The value perception of the products in every case is quite different. The value perception of the consumers is also different.

The actual purchasers of the products are the buyers for the shops – the first tier. The client has used a firm of marketing consultants to research and ascertain the several types of buyers:

■ some are owners;
■ some are shop managers working on behalf of the owner;
■ some are of both of the above types but in addition have pretensions about buying only genuinely artist/sculptor designed items;
■ others want anything that sells quickly;
■ the department stores have buyers who are of several types too, buying to a prescribed specification, or buying to a personal performance-related target.

Buyers have a general interest that the products will sell to their customers and many specific selfish interests depending on the type of buyer they are. For example, an owner-buyer is able to make a riskier buying decision; buyers for a department store are mindful of the fact that they can be sacked if they make a mistake.

One client of a marketing consultant sells at exhibitions to buyers. A further sales process has been developed because buyers act in quite a different way from their normal buyer behaviour when at an exhibition. There is also the prospect of closing new buyers at exhibitions, which is quite different from selling to new buyers on their home territory. The products are then sold by the client's buyers to consumers in every case, who pay a retail price – they are the second tier of customers – in this case consumers.

Consumers again are a varied lot – all individuals – and the client has used the computer software package that the marketing consultant installed to analyse buying patterns. Unsurprisingly, the client finds that consumers purchase in different parts of the country in different ways and their buying needs vary according to the time of year. Consumers seek an outlet that matches their own buying needs. Where they are and the mood they are in when buying will influence their decision. If they are on holiday they are more generous and carefree and may remove the stricter buying process curbs they normally apply. If they are in a group, again buying behaviour changes and influencers play a greater part. Some towns have a dominance of a particular consumer. Some designs are collected as sets. The overall UK economic state affects gift purchase with purely decorative items selling well when times are good and more practical useful items when times are harder. On the marketing consultant's advice the client ensures buyers are made privy to the consumer analyses as a customer relationship generating activity.

Understanding the customer may take time to become really effective. A new business would have none of this to use and other activities need to be undertaken to overcome this hurdle.

In summary the 'customer needs process' has to be carried out twice – once for each tier; but for each tier there are also subsections of customer types that may require further analysis and separation – known as segmentation.

So now the different types of customers have been roughly separated into segments. How do we store all the information and keep it all in mind just in case they call? You do not need to understand an infinite amount of detail about customers – though some database systems supplied for customer relationship management can now offer this facility. What you need to know is the information about the customer that is relevant to making a sale or relevant to you in that part of the sales process. You need to have that knowledge in front of you only when the customer is in front of you or is on the telephone to you. This is called 'knowledge management', the provision of timely and relevant information at the moment you need it – more of this later.

Recognizing that even a seemingly simple customer overview is quite complex to analyse is helpful for understanding marketing. To help sell to that customer further understanding of the customer is required.

Thinking from the customer's viewpoint

People end up with so much baggage from the cultural and social environment of their upbringing, their education, their life experience that it is easy to make assumptions about how others think and are likely to respond to communications with them.

Accept the fact: the people you are selling to are unlikely to be from the same cultural, social, educational, life experience background as yourself. Take this fact as really important. If not, you may have a problem grasping the need for marketing and the rest of this chapter.

It is easy to assume that one target group of customers is much like another and despite research for which you may have paid, in real life, your own people (even perhaps yourself) may ignore that research and apply what they have done before – because it is easy, because it's easy to plead that it worked before, because... Everyone has such convincing reasons.

Example of failing to use market research

Estates Gazette in October 2000 (in an article by Kim Tasso) reported that estates agents apply the tried-and-tested campaign formula of 'let's produce a brochure, run a few ads in the main property magazines and maybe send a promotional flier to the people on our mailing list'. This is done without any recourse to the original research, strategy or target market.

For every customer segment that you decide to select as a target (you do not need to target every segment, equally technically you could target every individual customer) you should apply the following procedure just before you start the analysis:

■ erase from your mind your own thinking and prejudices;
■ learn to listen, observe and grasp how your target thinks, communicates, comes to conclusions;
■ understand what makes the target tick, react, and so forth.

This method has been described as self-recognition criteria – accepting that the way you think and react is certainly wrong for any target you are analysing. You should not make any assumptions about the target customer.

Now that you have an open mind about customers, let's find out and consider what makes them tick and how they express their needs.

Marketing traditionally considers the needs of the customer in terms of four 'Ps':

■ the product or service;
■ the place;
■ the price;
■ the promotion.

(Others add 'Ps' for 'process', 'people' and 'physical evidence'.) The author considers that this approach gives the wrong perspective for the analysis of the marketing needs of the customer and the subsequent decision making about the marketing activities to apply. It is a sales-staff-needs-led list.

It is better to approach the customers' needs (whether the customers are buyers or consumers) *in terms of their view* of the four 'Ps'.

Actually, what you are really doing is applying self-recognition criteria – looking at the 'Ps' – from the customer view. And when you do this, the four 'Ps' become six 'Cs':

■ Cost – a customer considers cost (and cost of ownership as part of that consideration).
■ Convenience of buying – a mix of place/location, opening hours, cash/cheque/credit card acceptability.
■ Concept – a mix of product and service – few products are sold without some sort of aftercare service.

■ Communication – how well the product or service is communicated to them.
■ Customer relationship – that formed between customer and the seller – CRM principles apply.
■ Consistency – the reassurance of ongoing quality and reliability of the other five 'Cs' – brand surety if you like.

Examples of the application of the six Cs: easyJet

Richard Branson's Virgin brand and Stelios Hara-Iaonnou's 'Easy' brand both offer a series of perceptions and images that cover a range of products and services. Stelios openly acknowledges his great regard for Sir Richard Branson. Take a look at one product/service – easyJet.

The six Cs are carefully applied.

easyJet is a mix of product and service – the *concept*. The Web site is promoted heavily in the London area – on London Transport and in the *Evening Standard* – often with incentives. *Communication* of the benefits is excellent. The earlier you book the cheaper it is, getting more expensive as the plane fills up. The booking procedure – online preferably, and there is an incentive as it is cheaper to book online – is a six-step process taking you through from flight selection to payment. It takes just a few minutes. No tickets are issued; you just have an e-mail confirmation. Booking in at the terminal is fast and there is no fuss. You pay extra for food and drink on the flight – but that seems more individual. The concept is popular. It is *convenient* in all aspects, you can book from anywhere with Internet access. It is low *cost* compared to conventional fare tariffs. The whole is well *communicated*. You get what you expect – no surprises. *Customer relations* are good. It is certainly *consistent*. At every stage the process matches the customer needs for the 'six Cs'. In consequence easyJet has many customers that have a bonding with them.

The above was written before the easyJet crisis at Christmas at Luton. That was a failure of contingency planning when a supplier failed – failing to de-ice the easyJet fleet of aircraft. The customer benefits from applying the six Cs still apply and the customer bonding formed with easyJet has continued unabated despite that setback.

Understanding how branding works for a customer

Customers are attracted to a 'concept' usually by their perception of the corporate brand. Customers retain perceptions and images and their own key senses trigger a brand if the retention has been successful. But beware, if the concept you are selling does not match the perception and image and experience of the customer, you are far less likely to make a sale.

It is quite possible to have different perceptions of your brand in different parts of the globe or even in different parts of the same country. Guinness for a time advertised unwittingly in Africa using a symbol that suggested that Guinness improved fertility. Brylcream was thought to be a food delicacy in another African country.

It is also quite possible to reposition a brand. Sometimes this is essential to save a brand that has become dusty and failing. Failures are often the seedcorn of success if the lesson is understood.

Examples of different brand perceptions of the same concept and how a brand can be changed

Lucozade was known in England, Scotland and Wales as an expensive convalescent drink sold in a distinctive orange cellophane wrapper. In Northern Ireland as a result of a chance favourable opportunity to advertise extensively on Ulster television it became the soft drink of choice. It was drunk by people like lemonad; it was drunk as a hangover cure; it was also a mixer with Bushmills and other spirits. The potential to sell it as a healthy drink was then realized and it was then branded as a sports health drink and sold throughout UK in a trendy can. The rest as they say is history.

Recently (in 2000) Pringle sweaters were in the doldrums and the future looked bleak. They had been sold using the same golfer to promote them for 20 years and with traditional designs and a flagship shop of ancient vintage in Savile Row. A decision to reposition the brand for the young involved total redesign in colours and finding new but related patterns. Extensive research to find out what had to be done so the new market would wear them was carried out. New designs retaining just a few links with the old brand through logo and pattern elements were created. A new modern-looking flagship shop and office were opened. The new England football team captain David Beckham has been wearing one of the new designs at an autographing session and so the brand may well be on the road to success.

How successful branding works

Imagine a picture frame about an arm's length in front of and slightly above your head. Hold your hands out and pretend to hold opposite corners. (Just do it – you won't look too mad!) The picture frame is blank until something fills it. Consider it as an extension of your mind. Now let us test your brand perceptions:

If you are told 'Coca-Cola', what image flashes into the imaginary picture frame? A particular bottle shape? The word 'refreshing'? Now think 'IBM'. Perhaps your imaginary picture frame is now filled with a word/logo or image of – a computer? (Research among lecture audiences shows most people put 'computer' into their picture frame.)

Assuming that you too thought IBM equals 'computer', is that a good thing for IBM? Well, no, actually. As that is not what IBM is selling nowadays. IBM is now selling 'business solutions'. IBM used to just sell computers – so the brand perception fails in terms of being beneficial to sales. IBM should consider giving 'IBM', as a name, to a computer firm and renaming itself something like 'Big Blue Solutions'.

Let us try the perceptions the other way round. What appears in your imaginary picture frame if we say 'Blackcurrant'? If you are in the UK, is it 'Robinsons' or 'Ribena'? This is where your selection may reflect your exposure to the media they use. But if you chose one or the other, they are in luck; you will probably head for their product as a preference, if you need to purchase blackcurrant. You have developed a bonding to a brand.

You may remember 'the listening bank' that did not listen. People didn't believe the branding as experience told them that the bank didn't listen. It was probably more of a strap line that went wrong. 'Midland Bank' has now been replaced by the 'HSBC' brand. If the experience does not match you will be more disinclined to purchase. This happens in practice and marketers do not learn. Barclays Bank were closing many branches in country areas to a great outcry while at the same time advertising themselves as a big, big global bank. Credibility is stretched.

Use the same picture-frame technique on 'Lever Brothers'. Here a firm has chosen to go for product branding rather than a corporate brand. You may not associate any products immediately with Lever Brothers. Your picture frame remains empty. Actually Persil is one of their products. Persil is very well known. But when they introduce changes to the product, they have a problem. Using a different name would be difficult and expensive to promote to reach the existing Persil sales levels. So they use additional words – 'new', improved' 'non-biological' to retain the product brand association – to keep the bond with the brand.

Does your company name appear in your customer's picture frames? If yes, you have a successful brand.

If not, you may need to call in a marketer. If you don't know whether you have a successful brand, a marketer will find out through customer research and then suggest the remedial measures so that your name does appear in your customers' picture frames – and you can measure that achievement through more research.

You may wish to play the 'picture frame' game given above for some time. The point is, if the brand association is instantly there and you have retained it in your customers' heads, it is a powerful sales supporter when the customer sets out to purchase. Analysts are beginning to recognize and measure this brand-bonding power as an intangible asset. It is a better long-term indicator of a firm's success than the financial trend picture.

How did the perception and image of a brand get there – the brand that you conjure up in your imaginary picture frame? It is a carefully considered process of effective marketing activity, probably involving drip-feed promotion over a long period of time. Equally it is possible to destroy a brand if it is not policed. To achieve a brand may not actually cost a lot. A programme of marketing activity is required, covering in an integrated way all aspects of the business operation and marketing communications – advertising, PR, direct mail, and so on.

Hopefully, the power of branding for a customer has now been demonstrated. You can achieve it for your firm. You set a business vision that requires a particular image and perception – a brand – among your customers. From that is constructed a marketing objective to achieve effective branding. Whether you have 10 or 10,000 or 10 million customers, the task is just to get your brand – a name or a logo (think of MacDonalds 'M') or a mix of the two and all the associated perceptions and images – into their heads, to be summoned readily into the frame.

Example of small brand building – Helmsmen Limited

The author is one of three people who own Helmsmen Limited – a business consultancy.

The name Helmsmen was chosen for the company because the work done is typically to steer or navigate a client through a difficult period – a change in direction perhaps, or the introduction of a new vision and focus or equivalent; a new product launch or new company launch perhaps. The impression is to put across the Helmsmen consultant as someone who is not there to take over the client but rather to provide a skilled, qualified and experienced pilot to take the client organization through a difficult patch and then step aside, remaining available to be called on again when circumstances demand, just like a pilot does for a ship entering or leaving port.

A brief was written to describe what messages Helmsmen principals want clients to receive about Helmsmen. We want them to know we are:

- experienced;
- mature;
- creative;
- practical;
- responsive;
- thoughtful;
- original;
- quick to learn;
- broadly knowledgeable.

We want them to think that we are:

■ useful;
■ effective;
■ distinct;
■ harmonious.

We want them to feel:

■ comfortable;
■ confident;
■ reassured;
■ optimistic.

As a result we want them to believe that:

■ they will prosper;
■ their reputation will be enhanced;
■ their company/organization will benefit;
■ they will not be at risk.

The Helmsmen brand is mainly to stimulate repeat business and Helmsmen clients do just that – return. Whenever a change, a difficult patch lies ahead – call in Helmsmen. The Helmsmen consultant knows the 'vessel, the waters and the crew'. But the client always remains in charge – and the captain and the crew still carry out their work.

The main means used to promote the Helmsmen brand is visual, verbal and practical, during assignments.

How do you sell to the customer?

The customer follows a buying process that needs to be analysed and understood, and a sales process then needs to be develope (by marketing) to match it. If it is a two-tier market then two analyses and two solutions will be required to understand how you sell to the customer; one solution prepared for the buyer, one solution prepared for the consumer. If the tiers are themselves divided into segments then additional analyses and solutions will be required and for different sales environments.

The buying process

Assume there is a point in time at which a customer has a blank mind – an empty picture frame. Into that blank appears a need – which, as has been described, can be rapidly associated with a brand. If that occurs and purchase of the brand satisfies the need the process stops. The mind may, however, not think of a brand or indeed feel the desire to seek an alternative if bonding to a brand is not strong, or by way of variety or change the mind may decide deliberately to ignore a brand.

Once a need is established, then the buying process begins. For example, a life partner may say 'we need a new sofa and two armchairs'. Suppose no brand occurs in the 'picture frame' for a 'sofa and two armchairs' set; the mind then seeks alternatives such as the word 'furniture'. Assume a number of furniture outlets do appear – DFS, Courts, Ikea, Arding & Hobbs and the like. All have promoted their brands and related them to 'furniture'.

What happens next? Thinking begins, trying to specify, define and identify the parameters of the sofa and two armchairs set. Note that some people, without inspiration or imagination, may well action the next stage – a search – and then carry out the first stage. The specifying, defining and identifying process may consider any, a number, or all of the following:

■ the material;
■ the size;
■ should the sofa convert into a bed;
■ the colour;
■ the design;
■ the price range that is acceptable;
■ the set has a warranty;
■ the make;
■ to buy the set through some finance arrangement;
■ any additional cost of delivery, or is delivery free.

Friends and relatives are likely to be consulted or will offer opinions. These influencers can seriously affect the specification and their input and influence are considered in a later paragraph.

Next a search for a sofa and two armchairs takes place. This could start on the Internet or on a TV shopping channel or by examining brochures at home (such as Ikea) but consumers generally like to experience goods of this type – so visits take place. A number of local furniture shops, department stores, warehouse specialists will be visited – probably the ones that appeared in the 'picture frame' under 'furniture'. It is unlikely that any decision will be made to buy the first sofa and two armchairs seen. This kind of purchase is not an impulse buy.

Evaluation and selection occur from the moment the first sofa and two armchairs set has been seen. Some sets will be rejected as not meeting the specification, other sets will be identified as being of an unacceptable quality, wrong aesthetic shape and so on. The influence of the salesman can be significant by throwing in additional points of specification, usually related to positive factors about a set that he or she is keen to sell.

Once a decision to buy has been reached, the actual purchase takes place. Even at this moment a number of causes can delay or stop purchase. The process may require a contract to be signed and acceptance of a complex form containing terms and conditions in small print, which can stop a purchase. The acceptability of the means of payment may stop or delay the transaction. Until fairly recently Marks & Spencer and John Lewis did not accept credit cards. Problems may arise with financial loan or hire purchase arrangements, which may cause the customer to walk away. The speed of processing the purchase transaction may be important to the customer. A long queue in prospect or an unfriendly sales assistant may cause a customer to walk out.

The buying process does not stop at the purchase. A customer will monitor the performance and operation of the purchased product or service. Unsatisfactory aspects may cause redress to be sought in money terms or some other form of compensation. The legal rights pertaining to purchases and the warranty period may apply. If monitoring proves beneficial the customer will log the experience either to influence others interested in purchasing the product or service or for a repeat future purchase.

The sales process

The sales process is achieved by matching the buying process, applying the six Cs and ensuring the operation is easy and customer friendly. Forming a sales process is a marketing activity.

The importance of establishing links between businesses

Customers react more favourably when there is confidence in an organization and that they have some form of redress. The consumer receives this from the warranty – the guarantee that is backed by legislation.

In business to business that is almost certainly not enough. You should always consider establishing links at different levels of the business with your customer. It can be described as the 'rubber glove' theory. Interlock fingers between firms (the gloves), at all levels within the firm (the fingers) and make sure the links are difficult to separate (the rubber). It may happen anyway, particularly with service firms – but do not leave it to chance.

The principle is simple. At each appropriate level you should make sure a link is established. This should not just be encouraged or left to chance. It must be an instruction. When a contract is signed then agree and decide the need for more links. People should be nominated at director, manager, supervisor, foreman, even delivery and shop floor level. The two examples in the frame on page 48 illustrate the effect of the 'rubber glove' theory.

In a very small firm make sure another director or partner is

Buyer needs/process and how we match them

Needs/Process	Perfect response	Practical procedures
Identify, define, specify	Matches six Cs	Find out needs – match six Cs, qualify, check buyer proposition
Search	Fully aware of product/services and benefits at the right moment	Marketing benefits, offers; potential customer contact – knows where to look confirmed
Evaluate and select	Be helpful, reiterate	Give yardsticks
Purchase	Unthreatening Easy to say yes to	Clear, if any, contract terms
Monitor	All positive	Feedback Build relationship towards next purchase

From the buying process of the customer you match with a sales process for the sales staff.

Sales process

Point in process	Objective	Practical steps
Just become aware	Build relationship, fact find, qualify, do not try to close a sale	
Aware but not a customer	Obtain a sales opportunity – test close	Keep in contact Contact plan Put across matched benefits
Sales opportunity	Win sale	Find buyer detail needs – match six Cs' benefits. Try closing
Now a customer	Demonstrate correct purchase occurred	Feedback on performance

In an exhibition environment that sales process is modified.

Exhibition sales process

Point in process	Objective	Practical steps
Just become aware of brand and concepts	Qualify, fact find, build relationship Make offer open to the end of that day or the show – if you are first stand visited; send to competitors Ascertain buyer type – owner/buyer runner	Open with non-threatening dialogue – with everyone Deliver evidence of six Cs Ask questions, qualify If owner, test close If runner offer all literature
Aware but not a customer	A sales opportunity – test close	Deliver evidence of 6Cs.
Sales opportunity	Win sale	Find buyer needs, close sale
Customer	Demonstrate previously correct purchase occurred, show new items, close sale	Feedback on performance Keep in contact Contact plan Put across matched benefits

Figure 2.1 *Establishing the sales process from the buying process and buyer needs*

involved. This would normally be the senior partner or managing director for clients of other directors. In a solicitor's department the partner in charge of the department should make contact with all the clients whose matters are being worked on by fee earners in the department. Just one phone call is enough to establish links.

Forming links and maintaining them – using a contact plan – is a marketing activity.

Two examples of the 'rubber glove' links

The importance of establishing more than one link between the firm and the client is essential. It is easy to leave the salesperson to make a single link with the customer but it is unwise. More than one contact is essential in most businesses – especially where a small failure can lead to the loss of a client.

A fulfilment house client of Helmsmen fulfils direct mail order responses – typically for insurance or financial companies. The consumer sends back a completed financial form for a credit card or an insurance quotation and the consumer then receives a free gift – a pen, a torch, a wallet. A fulfilment house sends the gift and follow-up letter.

The client was tasked to send out a batch of letters to a precise timetable. They did not receive the draft in time but the salesperson was assured by the client contact that it did not matter. It did. They lost their top client for a period of 18 months, because the contact had lied when reporting back to their own superior that the draft was passed on in time. Fortunately a similar fault by the same contact brought to light another lie – and the contact was sacked. A chance meeting between managers led to re-establishment of the contract. This time contact was established at many levels. Working level, supervisor/manager level and at managing director/director level. This is the 'rubber gloves' link theory. Close links are established between two organizations like the fingers of two intertwined rubber gloves. Then when a problem occurs between two people you have more links to get round any one unsatisfactory link.

For a die-casting client – a cosy business where everyone knows everyone – similar links are essential. When a lorry load of castings arrives the driver has a quick word as they are unloaded (along the lines of 'all right mate'), a little later the die-casting foreman checks by phone with the floor supervisor that the quality of the die-castings just delivered is up to speed and so on. With no such links, if a fault is found there is no feedback to the supplier and a report is received internally up the management chain about a 'duff load of die-castings', even if only one or two are faulty. The matter escalates to manager level and rapidly the supplier finds they are no longer supplying die-castings. With 'rubber glove links' at all levels the matter can be nipped in the bud and replacement castings quickly arriving to replace the few faulty ones. The contract is safe.

Building relationships for repeat sales
Building relationships is important and should be encouraged. For relatively small effort a large number of repeat sales can be made. It is particularly important to make contact with those who have bought before in a timely fashion. A car dealer should ascertain the buying period between new car purchases of customers – often from historic data. Then as the time when a purchase becomes imminent, information about new cars, offers to view, invitations to test drive should be forthcoming. This is often the opposite of reality – when a person is inundated with mail just after a purchase but by the time a new purchase is about to be made – nothing is communicated. Building relationships is a marketing activity.

It is important to establish re-order frequency and match a contact call to that period. For a professional firm seeking new business it is even possible to ask how frequently contact should be made. It can be made into a process with a contact plan for each client. That is, persons in the team are tasked with maintaining contact at set frequencies and the type of contact decided. The process can be managed centrally using a database.

All contacts on a central database
There is plenty of software available (ACT and so forth), which allows a firm to make contacts according to contact plans.

Centralizing the database allows everyone to see who is the point of contact with whom. For professional firms the history of individuals and moves to new firms can be tracked. It is particularly beneficial to maintain contacts as they move up in hierarchies and move to new companies, which results in new business with the new firms to which they have moved. This is particularly beneficial if the brand values have been established in early years and the contacts are then tasked with finding a service supplier for the service you supply. This is particularly helpful for professional firms in a niche when the client merges with a similar body and one of the professional firms has to go. Maintaining relationships may just sway the balance in favour of the firm that is known to those at the top rather than the firm that has not built on relationships.

The knowledge management tool

Knowledge management can be used to provide timely key information or intelligence about a customer and the matched product/service to a salesperson. Knowledge management can be used for example for a taxi driver to pass on the knowledge of where (with timings) are all the concerts or football match crowds on any day. That knowledge could be shared with ambulance managers – allowing a plan at any time for optimal deployment of ambulances in a county.

Knowledge management can also be used to provide knowledge about a customer at the point of sale – to describe, say, the general pattern of purchases of that customer – and present the knowledge in a way readily understood by the salesperson just when they need it; when the customer is standing before them or is on the telephone and contemplating a purchase. For business customers the influencers can also be entered into the database and the information they need provided.

Example – knowledge management in the early days

In 1989 a client ran a Nissan car franchise in London. Half the business was new car sales. The other half of the business consisted of car servicing, maintenance, repair and carrying out services such as MoT testing, car cleaning and car valeting. The

Helmsmen task for the client was to make the non-sales side more customer friendly.

Helmsmen's market research showed that customers assumed that the garage knew all about their cars. We needed some way of providing service reception with knowledge about the car belonging to the person on the other end of the telephone. We applied a very basic program to solve the problem – computer programs were basic in those days – but it was sufficient for the purpose. Service reception keyed in the first three letters of the surname and a frame appeared describing the car, the last service/repair and when the MoT was due. Even in those days a courtesy car was provided to the owner for the period between the garage driver collecting and returning the owner's car.

Service business took off. Even when Nissan UK targeted this garage and put the client out of business in the Nissan scandal, his servicing business was able to carry on because of the strong relationships built up.

The part played by the influencer

Buyers, when they make buying decisions, are influenced by their positions within their own business environments. They worry about the attitudes of others to the decision they take: of their superiors, peers, subordinates, friends and family, to a greater or lesser extent. Marketing must seek and identify these influences, add them to the knowledge management equation and satisfying the buyer's needs with that understanding.

Buyers can be from within a business, buying on behalf of the owner. This introduces the possibility of many different people influencing the buyer and the buying decision that is made.

Buyers are influenced by:

■ Where is the buyer in the firm?
■ How does the buyer fit in?
■ To whom does the buyer report?
■ What are the office politics/culture/relationships?

Such information is readily stored on a computer database.

Competition

The first, possibly salutary, exercise you may care to carry out is to find out where you are in the overall market, the size of your market share in cash terms, outlets terms (distribution), position in the market, and so forth, and see what part you play in it. Now is market share important? If you are not the leader, is that important? If you are the leader is that significant? Answers in a moment.

It is a researched fact that the brand/product with the largest market share has a head start on the others. If you are No 1 then a lot of people will buy from you just because you are No 1. To remain No 1 you will have to do exciting and innovative work to remain there, but less than any competitor at No 2 trying to become No 1. In fact if you are not the top it is often better to invent a new category and be No 1 in that than to try to take over as No 1. Many firms have chosen to adopt a new category position particularly in a global market situation.

However can you be No 1 in less than a global market? Yes, you can. The concept of being No 1 is possible in local terms or as a specialist supplier (the new category). Think of a large town with a department store or the largest car showroom or the biggest local property developer. You can be No 1 in your area and it is worth getting there because, as they say, size matters – you benefit from being No 1. You can also be No 1 as the biggest supplier to a particular group of customers of a specialist product/service. You can be in a niche – the top supplier and No 1 there.

So how do you decide what to be No 1 of? Let's be practical. What is your capacity to be No 1? And of what?

First think in terms of your 'production' capacity and potential. You may have the equipment, workforce and factory space to produce goods that will produce, say, a turnover of half a million. If you are a professional service your 'production' capacity may be the total of the hours each of your professional fee earners can work, including their overtime – again say half a million turnover; that is what you have to sell. How many customers do you need to buy all your 'production'? Are your customers geographically based, or specialism based – with you providing a specialist/niche product/service? Whichever it is, think of them as your pool of customers. Your pool may be business customers or consumers. You will always have people in your 'pool' of customers trying out a competitor so your pool must be large enough to accommodate that. Perhaps you may realistically achieve 40 per cent market share of your potential 'pool', in which case you need a 'pool' size of two-and-a-half times your production capacity. That is your target market. If your percentage share is smaller, then you need a larger target pool.

Who else are suppliers to that pool? They are your competitors. You should be No 1 supplier either geographically or as a niche specialist.

Most firms do not have even a single figure percentage in global market share terms. So global market share does not matter – unless your pool is global. Less than a single figure global market share and you can consider yourself 'in the noise', but you are not alone; what matters is the position you hold in your 'pool', the pool of potential customers you need who are going to be buying your 'production', your 'service', your 'concept'.

You can be different and successful in other ways to beat the competition. But you only need to worry about competitors in terms of market share in your 'pool'. And to beat them you need the six Cs. Think in terms of each 'C' and how you can be better than each competitor.

Examples of being No 1 – city optician and county solicitors

Personal services retailer
A client of ours has only one outlet in London. It is not the leader in its market overall in the UK, which has many similar outlets. But it is really successful in that it manages to get three times more turnover from its one store than anybody else. This is well known in the client's catchment area. People use the service and buy products and services as a consequence. The firm and its customers are proud of it. The success comes from its marketing and retention of that position in its pool.

Although Helmsmen advised them to clone their concept across the UK, they turned the suggestion down; they were worried they would be dealing with people they don't know, that they may lose control and make less turnover per outlet, less profit overall. They were probably correct to ignore Helmsmen's advice. They make sufficient for their needs in terms of the bottom line. (Helmsmen understand that they are now to clone the operation after all.)

Family solicitors

Helmsmen researched most of a county for a legal client. They found that the market for family legal services was growing. The research also found that non-family legal services were unlikely to grow – the county planning regulations were against any new commercial or industrial growth. The market town is the centre for about a third of the county and this was decided to be the area in which they wanted to be No 1. Helmsmen advised on a six Cs-based programme of marketing including adopting a high profile in their market town base.

The result has been successful growth with more business and new offices in neighbouring towns, more fee earners employed – they became No 1 in their part of the county.

Interestingly a rival firm of solicitors asked to merge with our client, giving the reason as 'to exploit the commercial and industrial activity of the area'; it was clear they had not researched the market; Helmsmen knew there was no growth potential there. The merger eventually did not take place but the real reason emerged: two partners were retiring and wished to take money out of the business, but there had been a fall in turnover over recent years and there was insufficient cash in the practice... as a result of competition from our own client.

Careful selection of the size that you wish your business to be, the likely market share you need to be No 1 and what can be achieved by marketing activities following from marketing objectives help set the size of your target market 'pool'.

A Kogan Page book, *How to Beat Your Competitors*, by John Fisher is a guide to analysing your competitions' performance.

Finally there is the black economy. The Victoria & Albert

Museum in its brands exhibition (on as this book was being written, January 2001) has a gallery devoted to pirating, with many examples of copied goods. Some of the copies are as good as the originals. Intellectual property crime cost £8.19 billion in 1999 alone. The November 2000 issue of *Director* magazine gives 10 ways to fight back:

■ be aware of your legal rights;
■ support your trade association;
■ emphasize the continuity of your company;
■ ensure the security of your supply chain;
■ educate customers about the dangers of piracy;
■ build anti-piracy design into products;
■ co-operate in a common cause;
■ use hotlines to report suspicious behaviour;
■ add value by improving service;
■ back groups fighting the pirates.

Helmsmen's clients have found trade associations – even those expressly formed to defeat pirates – fairly ineffective. The best method is to build anti-piracy design into products.

MARKETING ACTIVITIES IN THE BUSINESS PROCESS

Marketing activities can help the firm at all levels and all points in the business process. Marketing activity helps in decision taking. Specific marketing activity can be commissioned in support of the business process.

The business process is dependent on marketing for the input to confirm that the market actually exists, its size and shape; this is at strategic level. This is where the application of the SMART criteria to business objectives has a marketing dimension.

Marketing can, from analysis of past data and assessment of trends, extrapolate/interpret that data to give an idea of the future. Marketing can provide measurement – statistics – from the previous year (sales by area, by product, by profitability, product range, customer numbers, and so forth). Marketing can sort out market segmentation and recommend the segments to target.

The application of marketing models and tools can help determine likely outcomes of market situations the firm is in, or may find itself in – giving support to the decision-making process as to which products or services to provide in the future and what in the way of marketing activities are needed in support.

Marketing can brief and direct market research activity. Key research activity is to seek out and identify future buyer behaviour and needs. Some of this can be desk-based research, which is usually fairly quick. Market research will also help with indications of customer product/service buying intentions.

Market research that listens can discover that which is normally unarticulated. To the marketer this is as precious as gold dust. See frame on 'unarticulated needs' below.

Marketing can also account for itself – if you believe in and use this book – confirming or otherwise that it is delivering value for money. A review of all the marketing activities should be undertaken to ascertain they give value for money.

Some marketing resource will be needed for this board-level support, which should be measured and costed. Each year some marketing resource will need to be set aside to carry out this activity.

Example of market research that uncovered unarticulated consumer needs – an adventure travel firm

A client in business for 37 years had been suffering from serious competition – could the situation be retrieved?

Carefully constructed customer research found that the consumers sought 'adventure', 'escape', 'a challenge', 'excitement', and so forth, all key words that are difficult to articulate in initial conversation with sales staff. Words that had not appeared in brochures or literature used by the firm. Others sought such achievements as 'to see Machu Picchu at dawn', 'visit Kathmandu'. Customer research also found that people from trips held reunions. Research of 10 years of records found 50 per cent repeats and referrals.

The sales staff were selling the benefits of the trucks: reliability of the vehicles, rare breakdown occurrences, airline seats, full first aid kit on board, full range of herbs and spices. These are all tangible features and benefits. They found it difficult to open conversations about the intangibles sought by the consumer.

The mismatch was resolved by introducing folding film-director type chairs with these unarticulated key words identified from the research, printed on the backs and fronts. The sales staff opened the conversation with 'I see you have sat down in "the escape" (or whatever), seat, is that what you are looking for?' Customers then found it easy to state the intangible they sought.

The trips (products) were changed to deliver the key words: for example the South American trip detours for a night on a salt desert to achieve 'escape' and those who have listed it as their reason are told on the night they camp there by the trip leader – who is now trained to do this – 'well done, you are farthest from civilization, you have achieved escape'. They are delighted that 'escape' has been delivered. The cost has been very low – just some market research and a few consequent changes. The benefit has been enormous – the right communication to support the sale and the value received on delivery is really appreciated.

Other communication was begun. A 5,000-km club was started. Mailshots were sent to former customers keeping them updated. The adventure travel firm goes from strength to strength.

Analysis of market research defines:

■ the preferred product/service characteristics;
■ the preferred method of purchase;
■ what needs to be communicated to support the sale;
■ the development of customer relationships – how best to achieve that;
■ how the brand is perceived with value perceptions; and
■ policing the operation to ensure consistency with the defined brand.

From this analysis, marketing activities can be generated to correct anything that is adverse or weak. This includes strengthening or defining more clearly:

■ corporate style;
■ corporate design – logo/policing of the design;
■ corporate messages.

The actual achievement is considered below.

Helping the operational side

The business process depends on marketing at operational level to help optimize efficiency and effectiveness through planning. Marketing objectives are derived from business objectives. A marketing plan is made up of marketing objectives that are both non-promotional and promotional. Each marketing objective, then, is achieved through division into a range of appropriate marketing activities. All the promotional and non-promotional marketing activities are then assessed for their success criteria. A way to measure that achievement is decided. Arrangements are described in the plan for using the measuring mechanisms and analysing them. These become part of the marketing activities themselves. Their cost is included in the marketing activity to which they refer.

Operational non-promotional marketing activities

Human resource

First, anyone responsible for a marketing activity is part of the marketing staff as we have described above. Second, if you adopt the first point made in this book – that you should measure all marketing activity – then as you are measuring achievement of each institutional activity, its achievement can be set as a part of or indeed a whole work objective itself for each member of your marketing staff. Clever. You can then get your staff both ways. If they do not suggest, recommend and implement marketing activities that work – towards achievement of your marketing objectives – they have failed. They must also choose appropriate mechanisms to measure achievement because if the mechanisms they choose are wrong they will be exposed. It will cause a much more careful culture in your staff in their selection of the best mix of marketing activities and thinking about the key performance indicator and its metric – the measurement mechanism and its appropriateness. It may also mean that they will be more honest before you commit any funds, saying that a particular marketing activity is inappropriate or underresourced or unlikely to achieve what you want.

In particular you are measuring the ability of your marketing staff to think through the marketing activity as a part of the achievement of a marketing objective and how success of that achievement – the key performance indicator – is to be measured both at the marketing objective level and for each marketing activity. If they recommend inappropriate marketing activities and inappropriate measurement mechanisms it will become clear that they are probably not the marketing people you need. However there is an important caveat – if you originally employed them to do something else and they are not trained in marketing or briefed properly on the business objectives and marketing objectives – it would be unfair to expect them to be successful.

Marketing staff: training and briefing

You would not employ someone untrained or unqualified as an accountant. Those you employ to undertake marketing activity should be qualified and trainied in marketing – and there are many courses and qualifications now available. You must also brief your staff on the business plan elements that they need to know that are relevant to marketing.

Sales staff: training and briefing

The same applies for sales as for marketing staff. There are plenty of opportunities for sales staff who are not closely supervised to find ways around the rules that they may be set for visits, for expenses and the sales targets they are given. They are particularly adept at 'milking' any incentives and optimizing, for their personal gain, any expense claim 'rules'. The section on scams gives some examples. Those you employ to sell may have an agenda to beat any system you establish rather than necessarily working just for your firm.

Merchandising staff

These people are quite different from sales staff. Once a sales-person has sold in, merchandising staff are invaluable where routine reordering for multi-outlet large organizations takes place. They are at the coalface. They also become adept at spotting early the points in a product lifecycle. They give early warning of failures of your delivery system. They are also a very useful check on sales staff if you gain their confidence. They are adept at spotting how individual buyers make decisions and allow the sales process to be refined and even individualized. Merchandisers can be checked through their client reorder records and from conversations with client buyers and sales staff and your own sales staff.

Product and service audit

Marketers need to routinely audit and check the status of existing products and the service provided to customers. Mystery shoppers can carry out a service audit. An audit of any services that are outsourced – particularly of delivery or fulfilment – is often eye opening. This is achieved by placing orders yourself and seeing how they are actioned. This is also a sound way of testing an intended service supplier. Routine product audits should be carried out monthly to spot early risers – products starting to sell fast, to discover where products have plateaued and when they should be discarded as they end their life cycle. A one-off audit is appropriate when deciding which products to support with marketing – point of sale or offers – to extend their life cycle.

New product development

Marketers should be involved in the research carried out and in defining future product parameters. They can advise on market research, testing, and provide answers related to preferred channels to communicate and distribution and price.

Operational promotional marketing activities

There are four main types of marketing objectives for which promotional marketing activities are considered.

Marketing activity to create awareness or educate

Marketing requires resource to create awareness or educate the target market. Marketing activities can be set to meet specified objectives. The purpose is typically to let people know about the products/services, their benefits and the sales outlets at which they can be ordered or purchased. Marketing activities here include advertising in all its forms, PR to obtain editorial comment and demonstrations to journalists, direct mail, Web site, e-mails.

Marketing activity to develop and sustain a brand
Marketing needs resource to cover perception and image objectives. The purpose is to support the brand, both on the product/service (concept) and corporate sides. Marketing activities will be similar to that above.

Marketing activity in support of sales
Marketing needs resource to produce a matching sales process to the way the buyer buys, which also accommodates any influencers, to allow ready purchase of products and services by the customer. This resource covers distribution and will include training of sales staff. To assist staff at the point-of-sale, provision of information on the buyer to assist the sales process – what used to be fact finding and has now developed into knowledge management. This could be a computer database with accumulated buyer information on it. There are other marketing activities that can enhance the sales process such as merchandising, incentives, point-of-sale publicity.

Customer relationship development
Producing a customer-relationships process, developing an ongoing dialogue with customers, which matches their needs – this is customer relationship management. The purpose is to retain customers so that purchases continue at the same or an increased level. This requires a database, and commitment from everyone involved to support a customer focus. It also requires information acquisition to build up knowledge management, applied to all customers and potential customers, and for staff.

The outcome of the process of marketing objective setting and designing marketing activities to achieve them is a marketing plan. The marketing plan is to accompany and complement the business plan. The marketing plan will also have a budget. The plan describes the reasons for the selection of the appropriate marketing activities.

There is also the need to manage, train and motivate those carrying out marketing activities such as:

■ the in-house operation;
■ training of all staff – on corporate objectives, focus, brand, feedback;
■ defining job descriptions and work objectives;
■ defining customer relations and management;
■ defining complaints procedures and handling;
■ data warehousing;
■ customer relationship marketing and viral marketing where appropriate.

There are also external activities:

■ advertising – selecting and briefing an advertising agency as to messages; confirming the selection of advertisements; commercials; affirming the methods of feedback as to effectiveness, overseeing campaigns and analysing the results;
■ direct marketing – selecting lists of target potential buyers, printing brochures, mailshots and so on;
■ public relations – selecting and briefing a public relations agency;
■ Internet communications.

Part 2

Marketing activities – description and measurement

This section is split into marketing activities that are non-promotional (Chapter 3) and promotional marketing activities (Chapters 4 to 7).

PROMOTIONAL MARKETING ACTIVITIES: INTEGRATION RULES OK

It is very tempting to follow historical divisors of 'above the line' and 'below the line'. In reality all marketing should be integrated and each marketing objective should be achieved through a mix of marketing activities.

Agencies that were formerly one or another type now realize that this is not helpful and offer a mix of both. Saatchi & Saatchi have realized that their key input is 'ideas' and they seek now to employ really creative people. Their output converts into marketing activities that are a mix of formerly above or below the line. An advertisement may direct you to a Web site. Spoof advertisements are currently in vogue; viral marketing works best (as at January 2001) – that is when individuals themselves pass on or alert others to your promotion. To capture the attention your brand, your Web site name should all be the same – integrated – and the use you make of all the media as seamless as possible, again 'integrated' is the word. Consistency makes people confident to buy. Even political parties lose their way through inconsistency, constantly changing policy and making U-turns, as they market themselves to the public. The consequence is that they then lose votes and of course elections.

The rise of direct marketing in all its forms is a reflection of the increasing ability to communicate with an individual through many media, including e-mail through the Internet. Computer databases make it possible to target individuals, hopefully matching their needs and allowing them to feed back views and information on products and services.

There has, however, been the introduction of very distinctive new media in recent years. At the time of writing, the Internet as a medium has probably been with us for six years, interactive TV about one year, the mobile Internet about six months. Because most people are still finding out how best to use them they are described here as 'new media'. However each of these should be no more than just a medium for communications and integrated into the marketing activities in support of marketing objectives. Just for the moment in this book they are kept separate to make their treatment clearer.

Many marketing activities rely on the use of a database or set out to create a database of interested potential customers or actual customers. The law covering databases in the UK and Europe is given at a number of Web sites. These are detailed in the references at the back of this book.

Finally it is appropriate to comment that the pace of technological invention does not stop and the next generation will have an impact soon.

As this is written, WAP telephones are now moving to a more mature stage of exploitation and being used to good effect by banks (one Spanish bank service put in a WAP operating bank service within 14 days) and by airlines (allowing customers to change their travel arrangements – rebooking on another flight for which they can ascertain seat availability).

For shopping list creation, you can enter the items you wish to purchase at any time from a particular supermarket in your hand-held device – downloading it as an order when you wish.

Future mobile phones will always have a facility enabling continuous two-way transfer of information – the downloads updating information held, particularly about the actual location the user is in. For example, this will allow you to ascertain the whereabouts of friends and colleagues in your locality at any time – say for meetings or lunch. This is scheduled for around 2003.

The new bias of technology is expected to increase personalized value-added, permission-based marketing communication in the future. Some believe this will lead to the marketer's finest hour, where marketing is built around the behaviour of people – going to where they are, to sell. The same people fortunately believe in the need to account for marketing – and to do that measuring marketing is the key.

3

Non-promotional marketing activities

This chapter examines non-promotional marketing activities. This includes measuring marketing persons.

If you find particular activities that you could classify both inside and outside marketing you should look carefully at them and take a firm decision to classify them as inside or outside, but do not keep them in both categories.

STAFF RESOURCES/OUTSOURCING STAFF

In-house staff

These are relatively easy to ring-fence and include within a marketing activity or a grouping of marketing activities.

Marketing staff
Marketing staff can be strategic planners taking input from sources including market research, sales statistics and forecasters. They can be market researchers, market analysts or marketing statisticians. They can be brand managers, product managers and at the other end customer relationship managers or anyone carrying out a marketing activity.

Each marketing activity for which they are responsible includes an apportioned share of their time and their costs. It is sometimes easiest to see what a person costs by looking in reverse and seeing what would you save if you did not employ that person and what activities would cease. This defines the cost and the activities to which that person's costs should be apportioned.

Sales staff

Here results are relatively easier to see. There are a number of sales control and recording systems available to buy for use with a sales force. Sales targets are set for areas or key account holdings or a matrix of product targets.

There are plenty of opportunities for ingenious sales staff to boost their earnings and expenses often quite legitimately by exploiting loopholes not foreseen in incentive schemes. Schemes that exploit or disadvantage customers can lose customers. A number of these are described in Chapter 4. When sales staff incentives are considered, time should be spent considering whether they can be exploited in ways not immediately obvious to non-salespersons. Specialist sales investigative expertise is available from a number of firms with vast experience of the sales scams that can be operated. Salespersons are not necessarily inherently inclined to find clever ways around incentive schemes. It is just that tradition has dictated that salespersons are only paid small salaries, relying on commission or other sales target-based schemes for their remuneration.

Merchandising staff

Merchandising staff are not there to make sales, but once a salesman has sold in a product range they ensure that reordering matches demand and that product displays and backup stock are maintained at set levels and reordering and supply occur just in time.

Merchandising staff are a useful way to measure the success of sales staff and their skill at selling appropriate stock for that customer. Sales staff are adept at enhancing orders just before they leave or are thrown out of a firm to the detriment of the merchandiser and the merchandiser is often the one direct link with the buyer that retains a client when a salesperson has overordered, incurring buyer and therefore customer displeasure.

Marketing communications staff

These are often included along with the other marketing staff. They are the staff that plan marketing activities and then oversee their implementation through agencies and contract staff.

Outsourcing – contract staff

Contract staff are employed through services: call centre staff (customer relations, telemarketing, customer response – order taking or brochure ordering), direct mail or fulfilment houses.

There are contract staff employed as an extra pair of hands. There is no reason why contract staff should be engaged other than with the achievement criteria of the tasks on which they are to work included in the contract. It is a human weakness often to engage temporary staff without specifying what they are to do other than a general generic description of a task – like giving a person a job description but without any work objectives. These people should be measured in the same way as your own staff.

Consultants can be engaged on a fixed-price basis to work on a task with the achievement criteria related to their payment(s). They, together with agency staff – PR, advertising, creative design and call centre staff – are considered in Chapter 4.

Measuring success of people

Generally, if the marketing activities are carried out and the measures for success you have set are achieved, then the people themselves have succeeded. The difficulties arise when you do not give single responsibility clearly for a marketing activity. Who does what has to be specified, so that the achievement of individuals is clear.

To see if you are achieving value for money in people you need to look at the success people have brought. Compare the achievement with the cost of those marketing activities and the cost of employing them. Again you may have to look at the long term rather than the short term.

For example, if your target was 40 new customers and your people found 40 new customers would that be success? Probably not in terms of short-term order values, say if the customers only became customers near the end of the period. They could bring long-term rewards in terms of purchases over several years, but not in a short-term view. You might initially be very happy if 50 customers were found but that happiness would fade if they all turned out to be single purchase customers only. This is why considering what to measure as success is essential when looking at the value of marketing. You would probably be happier knowing that the newly found customers all matched your long-term customer profile. But you would need to have measured that – both in your existing customers and the new ones to know that they matched the existing customer profile. More of this in the next chapter where the measurement of marketing activities is considered.

Take another example – a merchandiser. Their value in a fickle business such as greeting card sales, where buyers switch from one supplier to another, may be in retaining display footage where your cards sell. Their measure of success may be a mix of actual order values, but with customer retention as well. What is the cost of failure here? Selling in to a buyer to recover lost footage and the months without sales may be very difficult to restore – what is the value of that? Measure the value in reverse – how much you lose if you fail to keep an account. So for a merchandiser, a second measure may be account retention. A good merchandiser in the card business can both retain customers and even bring in 10 times the cost of employing them in order values.

Although market research staff should be measured in terms of the delivery of the marketing research activities – that is the information delivered – you should look for more. An element of their expertise is to select appropriate research methods and mechanisms that are efficient, effective, timely and cheap. If the information supplied does not allow decisions to be made then they are not successful. Equally you would not be happy if they spent a fortune finding an answer that is already freely available. So you may wish to measure their ability to select correctly the optimum solution to give you the information on which you can act.

Those responsible for external contracts should be measured in terms of the satisfactory performance of the supplier. Is that all you want from them? Perhaps you want early warning of any deterioration in performance. More than just monitoring, but early warning.

You may be able to measure customer services staff by the number of complaints or compliments you receive, particularly when delivering intangibles – say a service. They can also be measured by using secret testing – mystery shoppers. Set up a few fictitious potential customers for them to serve so that performance can be experienced. Your ingenuity in finding measures for people should know no bounds.

Measuring mechanisms for the performance of people

A job description gives a template for the kind of people you are seeking – what they may be expected to do and the qualifications, experience, knowledge, skills that they would probably have – and possibly an indication of previous achievements required for a holder of the post. These are not targets but just descriptons of the kind of person you require. Targets are set through work objectives.

The Investors in People appraisal system is a widely accepted scheme of setting down agreed work objectives, reviewing those objectives, then annually carrying out an appraisal of the achievement or otherwise of the work objectives.

The marketing activities for which an individual is responsible and their achievement can be included in any work objectives set for the individual. Measuring the achievement of that person is tied into the achievement of the marketing activities for which they are responsible. Sales is a marketing activity: achievement is typically measured by reaching or exceeding sales targets set for areas or key account holdings or a matrix of product targets. If a sales person fails to make sales – even after training – then you would eventually part company. The same would apply to marketing people – where they fail to deliver against work objectives, you part company.

Each marketing activity or group of marketing activities is set down in work objectives within an appraisal scheme. At the end of the appraisal period the person has either met the work objective, nearly met or not met the work objective. Rewards, promotion, salary reviews can be tied to success here; equally warnings, demotion, eventual removal can result from failure to meet work objectives. The work objectives are assumed to be within an appraisal scheme such as one recommended by Investors in People (IiP) in the UK.

Contractors' staff working for you through a service contract should include the marketing activities achievement as a prerequisite for part of the payment – if not all of it.

Marketing activities that are mainly of a service type will often be producing tangibles that can be assessed for achievement against the success target set – such as a report. Intangibles may require a third party to measure the deliverable – such as proving that a service occurs as set down. The use of mystery shoppers is invaluable here. There are companies that will carry out mystery shopping. It is often a salutary experience to follow a service provider through the process for which they are contracted.

OVERHEADS

Overheads? HQ, offices and equipment

Accountants like to apportion everything, including overheads. In some businesses headquarters staff are shared out proportionally, as are the cost of offices. Equipment, computers and the like may be charged to departments or pooled centrally. Whatever the policy at your business is, this is probably what you would wish to follow for costing purposes. This is important when giving single responsibility for marketing activities – and how overheads are apportioned.

Again it is sometimes easier to see what a person, team, section or department costs by looking in reverse and seeing what you would save if you did not employ them. If you are starting from scratch, as a rule of thumb the total cost of employing anybody is double their salary.

When totting up the cost of any marketing activity you will need to add such costs as your firm dictates that apply to all departments. Perhaps there are no measurements of success criteria to worry about here. Or are there?

If your customer relationships are important you may need to consider the benefits of investing relatively small amounts of money in modern equipment to enhance a marketing activity – something that is usually costed as an overhead. The cost of any telephone equipment/exchanges, say with call logging, may be a centrally based and costed item. The effect of poor experiences of customers trying to call you may effect sales. You may wish to find out and measure the ability to make inbound calls. You should regularly test all your customer response lines.

Examples of telephone mismanagement

Staff at one high street bank admit the call number printed on their bank statements is left permanently off the hook – because it rang too much. The call centre staff at this particular bank, while very helpful, give out a series of telephone numbers that no longer exist, have become fax lines, or are transferred to telephones that reconnect you to the call centre – from where you start again. This is a poor state of affairs in terms of customer relations. It is an area where measurement would sharpen up those responsible.

BT Cellnet customer service offers a series of four or five options, four or five times before a human operator is found. This is a frustrating experience but pressing five zeros in a row, one concerned customer services person says, will help you avoid the hassle and get to a person.

World Books answering service was circular for a time: you could never find a person to talk to – the automatic response system fed the enquirer back to the start of the loop

---

For a small firm wanting to seem a larger organization than they are, then the purchase of some of the latest telephone answering machines might solve the problem. Buying an appropriate machine allows a small firm to appear to have many extensions. People perceive you as larger when multiple choices are offered when their call is answered. This can be helpful to separate sales calls from queries about maintenance, when a salesperson calls in to pick up their messages. This opportunity to automate needs to be balanced against the irritation of customers if the process takes too long.

Modern exchanges often have facilities to store details of all calls made in and out – alternatively a detailed statement can be ordered. This is a source of additional and sometimes valuable information on the performance of any marketing activity that uses a telephone line.

Office machinery other than telephone exchanges, such as

computers and printers, may also be centrally controlled. However it is possible to purchase appropriate equipment to save on the cost of a marketing activity. The advent of desktop publishing along with the price drop of some printing and camera equipment means it is now possible to justify printing in-house small quantities (say less than 5,000 copies) of material – it is cheaper and very much faster. This means material can be updated or personalised every time. It means you can test out ideas in-house before giving the larger run to a printer. Double-sided A4 full colour laser printers are less than £2,000 (as at January 2001). Professional digital cameras under £1,000. The computer with a sufficiently large memory capacity and software is probably just over £1,000. If you use a commercial digital printer subsequently, then the material for printing can be supplied through the Web or on disk (CD ROM) again saving time. It is worth paying a visit to a commercial digital printer just to see how compact (even with lacquering) a digital press is – no larger than a small broom cupboard. To contemplate the 10 terabyte memory that it has is mindboggling. As an example, the time to type in, produce and print an 8-side A4 newsletter in full colour with photographs can be less than a day using a commercial digital printer.

Another possible saving, but using conventional litho printing, is to use a 'gang' machine, which prints personalized mailings from computer onto headed paper, prints addresses and any messages onto printed envelopes, folds and stuffs the mailing and any inserts into the envelope, seals the envelope and then franks the envelope with the appropriate postage. Preparing mail for mailsort is also a possibility. Such a single pass 'gang' machine – the speed of the service set against its cost in terms of capital and maintenance – should be compared with your present method. For example, an organization that offers to print in-house and quotes two to three weeks to send out a mailing for 4,000 – because a lot of the process is carried out by hand – may well mean that customer relations are adversely affected. Volumes of mailings should also be considered as a factor. A typical 'gang' machine can produce 22,000 pages an hour, every hour of every day.

Examples of fast and slow response

First Direct bank is now able to get letters out to customers within a day – for example letting them know of overdraft limits being breached.

Compare that with BT where for a client it took eight letters of complaint to Oftel and about five months to get a written response to a billing query.

Overhead and equipment costs and whether they should be included in any marketing activity will normally be subject to the firm's accounting rules. It is worth querying though, any overhead or equipment where it impinges other than favourably on the performance of a marketing activity.

Difficulties with what to include as marketing

If you are in doubt and the activity is something to do with customers, it is probably a marketing activity. You should give single responsibility for it accordingly.

Those of your staff whom you do not require to be trained to deal with customers should have an intermediary who is a trained person as their point of contact. Some form of Chinese wall should be used to keep the untrained staff apart from customers – or you may well discover some process or practice you wish to keep hidden from customers is revealed. You may allow a customer to speak to accounts for example, although even this may be unwise. You should measure how often this happens in any case. You may have a customer relations problem.

On the other hand if you train all your staff about customers then you will find that they react well to the occasional query and will respond to customers positively. Customers also pick up that your team is all working together.

Example of positive staff reaction to customers

As a former government inspector the author found the 'shop floor' always tells you everything and effectively produces the

> report. Staff actually want to see the customers being well served and are unhappy if they see them being short-changed or poorly served in any way. Staff are particularly unhappy if they have been told to treat customers in an unfair way or they have been ordered to cut corners in the manufacturing process.

IBM places great store on business-to-employee (B2E) communication in the future as a source of improved performance and customer focus. If employees are not customer focused, then most probably they are not working together towards ultimate customer satisfaction. The choice, as they say, is yours.

CONCEPT (PRODUCT/SERVICE MIX)

The product part of the mix may not seem to be related to a 'marketing activity'. The actual production, that is manufacturing, assembly, finishing and testing indeed is probably not related to marketing. There may be inputs as to colour and trim meeting a customer's particular specification. But generally the actual making of an item is not part of any marketing activity unless you are a 'hand-made' process where, as part of the PR/sales process, you allow customers to view the product being made. Health and Safety regulations may preclude much more than viewing. Pottery decorating, weaving, craftwork are typical examples. Sometimes it is important not to show manufacturing processes that may give the lie to perceptions built up about how a product is made. There is also the risk of competitors discovering the secrets of production processes.

Marketing activities that relate to the concept, the product service mix, are as follows.

New product development (NPD)
Here research and feedback of customer needs are essential:

■ Market forecast inputs relating to the economic environment; for example gift items, need to be more practical in times of recession but can be purely decorative in buoyant times.

■ Market movement – trends – in volatile markets such as fashion can mean feast if the predictions are correct or a time of famine if not. (Ask Marks & Spencer about getting fashion right.)

■ Defining the service elements related to the product – there are some service elements to every product. There are very few pure services: most include a tangible element as well.

■ Historical inputs from customers relating to past product service satisfaction – these can be indicators of future customer behaviour. Customers themselves can be analysed as innovators, early adopters, average purchasers or followers who only buy after the rest of the target market.

■ Forecasting the customer view and likely takeup of new products can be determined using models of customer behaviour.

■ Assisting with the management of innovation. Many new products never see the light of day. Some products are introduced too early before the market is ready to receive them.

■ Defining the production/service capacity – to match to the promotional marketing activity later. It is unhelpful to overdo the marketing activity when production cannot match supply to the demand.

■ Market research and the setting up of customer panels to help with the development and research for new products can be achieved by using specialist firms or by placing invitations to participate on existing products (see Chapter 3) and by including questionnaires with existing products (see Chapter 7).

■ Measuring mechanisms for some of these marketing activities are included in Part 6. Others can be resolved using market research (see Chapter 7).

Existing product reviews

Marketing activities applied to product reviews generally use a number of marketing tools. Marketing tools are normally best left for qualified marketers – chartered marketers – to apply on your behalf. Three are mentioned here:

■ *Where is the product/service in the product life cycle?* This information is obtained from database records of sales patterns. It is possible for the life cycle to be at different points in different markets. This will give an indication of the production requirements for the future. It may assist in making pricing decisions – offers such as three for the price of two and promotional decisions to raise flagging demand.

■ *What should you do with each product/service?* The Boston Consulting Group uses a matrix – a visual decision-making aid – in which it is possible to place each product/service and as a result determine an indication of the promotional activity that should be applied.

■ The use of the Ansoff Matrix can help decide which products or services to plan to sell to whom.

Measuring mechanisms for these marketing activities are included in the advanced section (Part 6).

COST (PRICE)

Customers consider the cost of a product when considering a purchase. That may be in comparison with similar products/service, it may be in terms of whole-life cost rather than just the purchase, it may relate to their perception of the status that ownership of the product/service imparts.

Cost is the value perception of product/service by the customer that will determine whether a decision is taken to buy or not. Price is the figure at which you, as supplier, may wish to sell – but, to customers, that is in many ways irrelevant to their purchase decision. Setting a price for a customer should be based on the value they attribute, rather than any cost-plus formula. Starting from scratch it is best to follow the leader in the market – but not always so. Brave entrepreneurs do look for cartel operations such as airline travel and start from a market-led basis; in the case of airlines filling every seat but at different prices depending on how early the seat is booked.

Some marketing authors try to define the customer view of value as: 'value is perceived quality divided by price'.

The customer value acceptance point is a basis for establishing the cost for many retail sector products and services. For example, to find out the figure at which you as a supplier will need to sell to a retailer, a typical cost-setting exercise will start from a cost point at which the customer will buy the product from the retailer.

Research finds the acceptable figure at which the customer values the concept. Taking that acceptable 'cost-to-the-customer' figure – usually a figure that is just below a round figure of a bank note or notes denomination or just below a digit increase (below £10, or £100 or £1,000 or £10,000) – which is known as a price point. From that figure work backwards including paying for any VAT in the calculation, to find the sum at which the retailer is prepared to purchase the item from the supplier. In straightforward logic, for 17.5% VAT, as a rule of thumb, many retail items in the non-food-and-drink sector will be bought at a price from the supplier that is then sold at 2.35 times to the customer to match a price point.

There are three price-based market activities in which measurement can have beneficial outcomes:

■ *Price changes.* Price movements up and down need to be carefully managed. How price rises are managed is the key to keeping customers. Again this requires a professional, a chartered marketer, to advise on how best to time and manage price rises. Price cuts should be similarly managed for maximum advantage in the market. Timing of a price cut can spoil competitor activity. Customer attitudes are affected by cost changes. Market research is best used to measure and assess attitude – see Chapter 7.
■ *Push or pull sales.* The use of push or pull sales tactics is often related to long-term or short-term objectives. Technically the term relates to the way you approach the distribution channel. If you want traders to stock an item you may give them incentives to do so. Alternatively if the marketing activities are such that every customer asks for your concept, eventually the trader will stock it. In sales tactics terms, push selling is a short-term tactic usually achieved by offering cuts in the price. Here the margin is cut to achieve this. This is a legitimate tactic to drive competitors out. Selling one item at a cut price as a loss-leader to attract people to buy other products is also legitimate. Usually such a tactic cannot be sustained as the long-term viability of a business may then be affected. Cutting price may also be used to sell stock that is at the sell-by date or where stock has been slightly damaged, and so forth. Fashion outlets use sales to clear old stock. Interestingly, for some people the value equation does not add up if a price is too cheap and the

potential customer will resist the opportunity to buy even branded goods that are offered at below the value point.

In the case of a pull sale, marketing activities pull the customers to the sale, usually over a period of time; this will include building up a relationship and will probably be heavily service orientated. Education, consultancy and pre-sale technical advice may be all offered free, as early enticements, to eventually secure a sale. These enticements are offered alongside normal marketing activities.

■ *Impulse purchases.* If you have a product that is an acceptable impulse purchase usually based on a customer value figure, then it requires special consideration. Being in an appropriate format in the right place at the right time (see below) when people are likely to have the money and the inclination to buy are key requirements for success. Any promotional marketing activity must consider this place and time imposition too. A street market deals in cash, as do car boot sales. The limit at a car boot sale in cash terms is probably around £500 (year 2001 estimate). The inclination to impulse buy may relate to the weather – selling umbrellas when it rains, souvenirs in the correct colours outside football matches. Also people are more inclined to buy when in holiday mood and this may cause them to override their normal value criteria. Selling items as impulse purchases on a routine basis requires a substantial footfall or crowd to pass by the sales outlet. London mainline railway stations see 200,000 typically passing through in a day. Socks, underwear, ties, flowers, chocolates, fast food and drink are classic impulse purchase items sold on mainline concourses. A client of Helmsmen sells inflatable swimming pools as a sideline to his main pools business at car boot sales, by telephone, but only in the summer and only on hot sunny days.

Measurement

Some appropriate measuring mechanisms for marketing activities connected with cost are included in the advanced section. However it may be an idea to create some measurements that are specifically tailored to cost issues. It is relatively simple to see changes in sales using monthly sales returns figures for each concept – product/service – if you want to see the impact of cost on customers buying habits. The same applies to weather-related product/service sales. You would need to record the daily weather against sales, and then you could forecast daily sales based on weather forecasts. How many people have made or lost fortunes running events on days when the weather impacted heavily on the outcome? Ask any seaside trader! Ask those who waited in Cornwall for the chance to make their fortunes during the eclipse! The opportunities for creating measurements are endless. If you are offering a loss-leader then achievement must surely be of sales exceeding the cost of the loss-leader. But how do you find out? You measure it.

CONVENIENCE (PLACE)

Convenience has become a priority in the customer's view. Convenience is an amalgam of:

▇ place – how easy it is to get to, park at, what is the speed and quality of customer service provided;

▇ the purchase facility – how easy it is to make the purchase transaction (credit card, cash or account) matched to the customer choice;

▇ time – opening hours, the ability to buy at a time suited to the customer need or whim;

▇ delivery of the concept – the product/service – if not immediate, at a suitable time/place and mode.

The variations of convenience are now becoming complex. The places where it is convenient to buy anything are changing all the time. At one extreme, now well established, there is the use of the Internet or interactive TV from home or from a mobile phone, with delivery to home or anywhere at any time.

Service stations that used to sell just gas/petrol/diesel now are small multi-line outlets for most daily commodities, a range of housewares, garden items, leisure products, as well as vehicle-related items and open all hours. Supermarkets/superstores now sell gas/petrol/diesel; they also sell clothing and other leisure and gift items and some (like department stores) sell appliances. There are seemingly no limits to what is selling where, or when, as long as it is recognized as convenient.

Of key importance to a new business that requires a heavy footfall, is to examine the most appropriate location for setting up. Also to research, if any changes to the concept are needed to be made in that environment. A client of Helmsmen was keen to establish a new impulse-purchase-related business. The client agreed to carry out market research to ascertain the footfall from the alternative routes from an Underground station to a tourist location to establish the best site – the research confirmed the unsuitability of sites on offer and also ascertained the number of people succumbing to an impulse purchase at a not dissimilar competitor operation. On this the client had a basis for a viable operation – but only along the main route. A major refurbishment of East Croydon railway station routed the footfall for a few years past a seemingly favoured site; the footfall has since dropped as a result of completion of the work and the advent of the tram system. Helmsmen's advice to the client saved a potentially hazardous investment.

Logistics

Logistics is a key element of convenience in that the supply of the concept (product/service) is part of convenience. This may require the ability to supply the concept for viewing. It may be the follow-up of the transaction, fulfilling the sale with a delivery of the concept – product/service – in timely fashion (at the time convenient to the customer). Convenient viewing and delivery are now accepted by customers as the norm. Failure to meet the logistics challenge can mean the difference between staying in business or folding. A failure of logistics has been a cause of dot.com failures. It is an operational activity that has marketing implications if it is not a seamless process; logistic consideration must meet the customer perception of acceptability.

Stock

Adequacy of stock to meet the actual demand level at any time is a second key element of convenience. The need to have assured stock levels and access to a ready supply to cope with demand is a part of convenience. Stockholding is anathema to accountants, who prefer no stock to be held. It is now possible to minimize stock and to re-order from a supplier automatically as the item leaves the retailer as the sales transaction takes place when the bar code reader registers the item as sold. In practice this information is stored into convenient batch sizes of data for transmission at predetermined times, but certainly at least daily. Patterns of demand can be established and supply matched to maintain stock levels. Stockholding reviews result from analysis of demand, turnover and stock checks. The supermarket chains and petrol retailers are becoming efficient at forecasting the likely demand levels in advance. They are alert to food programme ingredient demands, they watch food hygiene and animal health stories, they watch the weather.

Examples of stock failure and success

Fast food prestige sandwich outlets at Canary Wharf were caught out when adjacent high-technology goods shops opened offering bargains. The stock of sandwiches ran out and they were unable to resupply in time.

A pub adjacent to the new stadium in Cardiff took over £80,000 in a few hours by correctly anticipating the thirst and rate of consumption of rugby supporters.

Distribution

Where there is an indirect route of supply of the concept – the product/service – to the customer, distribution plays a part. The distributor or distributors offer benefit in that they market, sell and hold a buffer stock in customer-convenient surroundings, but there is a cost as each link in the chain adds a charge to the cost of producing that convenience, all of which is paid for by the customer. However the customer has the ultimate say in that if the cost is too high – beyond their value perception – they may refuse to purchase. Practical convenience dictates that distributors will remain a preferred customer source for a long time. The alternatives of buying directly and receiving directly products/services – the concept – from the manufacturer or supplier are still being developed. Some of the problem relates to the need for someone (at the home of the customer) to be in when the delivery takes place.

Measuring mechanisms for these marketing activities are included in the advanced section.

4

New media

This section covers the Internet (e-mail and the Web); mobile Internet; and interactive digital TV marketing.

Should you use the Internet, mobile Internet or interactive TV, or all three?

In fact, business-to-business use of the Internet is growing strongly (as at January 2001). As a selling tool, a Web site shortens the time and reduces the cost of procurement. It may be the channel for the conduct of most business purchases in the future. At the office, during working hours, the person sat in front of the PC is also a consumer and is likely to make forays onto Web sites to purchase items. Not all firms allow this and a recent circulation of a private e-mail may cause further restriction of Internet browsing by large or professional firms. Firewalls are being used to protect businesses from e-mails that contain pornographic or other unsuitable material. But the Internet is probably a must for the future for business to business but also for consumer purchases during business hours by business working consumers. It is also possible to put over more information on a computer screen than on interactive TV.

At home the Internet, despite a forecast 25 million users in the UK in 2005 (from 16.5m users in February 2001) is less likely to be used in the future – recreating the office environment in some room away from the family with a PC is probably less enticing than using the TV in the living room. Interactive TV is forecast to have 19.6 million users in the UK by 2005. The technology potential and existing 'in-home' presence of the television is forecast to make interactive TV the preferred marketing activity for business-to-consumer communication in future. Forrester Research forecasts that, by 2005, more Europeans will be using interactive TV than going online to use the Internet. Forrester forecast that, in 2005, 5 per cent of retail sales will be online – half-Internet and half-interactive TV. In the United States, always a year or two ahead of the UK, the growth rate of use of the Internet is slowing down (as at January 2001). In 2003 Europe will have overtaken the United States in both Internet and mobile phone use. In the UK nearly 20 million are Web-enabled now, with about 10 million active on the Internet. The most used sites attract some 600,000 unique visitors a month. (Tesco and Railtrack). Few sites achieve more than 200,000 a month. Sainsbury's find Web transactions are four times the average in-store order.

The mobile Internet is primarily being used by the 18–24 age group and usually in connection with entertainment, lifestyle and leisure. If your concept matches this age group and those activities then you should consider the mobile Internet – there are excellent introductory (cheap) offers on now as this book is being printed.

Are the new media any different from the old media? Charlie Dobres, co-founder of I-level, the UK's second largest specialist agency operating in the new media sector, says no. He says that, if anything, most marketers will find they need to go back to basics. Ninety-five per cent of what you need to know for the new media, any marketer should know. Five per cent is technical or jargon. It is not a new economy in marketing terms.

Charlie Dobres believes you should look at a Web site as a shop. You would not expect people necessarily to buy first visit, or even on the second visit. He quotes research by QVC as indicating that some 90 hours viewing occurs before first purchase. Counting 'click-throughs' or 'hits' as a measure of success of a Web site is a waste of time, all you are recording is shop entries. For example, some define a hit as a viewing of a link or graphic; so a visit to a page with 10 graphics and 10 links would be recorded as 20 hits. Recording an arrival on your site is a measure of the success of your advertising that got people to the Web site in the first place. Particularly if it is related to time. A weekend advertisement in print or on TV or cinema screen would bring visitors at the weekend and on Monday morning.

Registration is a better measure of Web site success as it shows an intent towards more involvement. Actual sales are, of course, the really persuasive measure of the success of a Web site.

Paul Cheesbrough of the BBC says that the role of marketing is to ensure fluidity and address the needs of customers – the interface between the organization or firm and the marketplace across the old and new media. He believes that the new media may not suit all brands. A question that should be addressed first is: is your brand right for the new media? If it is not then ways around this may be to co-brand or rebrand. The real appeal of the new media is the quick response time it allows and the real-time operational facility.

Example of using the new media

Abbey National operates a fully integrated multimedia marketing operation.

Ambrose McGinn, retail e-commerce and strategic development director, says Abbey National has based its marketing on the achievement of a single branded customer experience with a mid-market family focus. This focus is age 30–40, married with children and with worries about technology, PCs, and schooling. They are also cash and time poor. The brand is developed to provide a straightforward 'can do' personality offering real and perceived values that Abbey National is flexible, fair, and gives an easier time and a more emotionally rewarding experience for financial services and banking.

Abbey National believes that its customers trust it, not technology. They believe in making customer life easier. This means Abbey National has moved into convenience retailing with banking services sharing facilities in Safeways stores, shopping malls and cafes where they can relax. At the same time, in those same places, they offer, alongside staff and cash machines, the chance to try out telephone banking, WAP phones, the Internet and interactive TV communications links with Abbey National. Thereafter they can use the links from office or home. Ambrose McGinn says 'they provide a consistent customer experience wherever they touch us each time'. Abbey's busiest time of banking is at 7.59 pm. It has found that it has to provide enormous capacity between TV programme screenings, when customers choose to communicate.

The result overall for Abbey National has been gratifying. Tests show a 40 per cent response on outbound marketing. They believe – and the evidence is accruing – that their return will in the long term be a greater share of wallet from the services they offer. They already are experiencing a 2 per cent unprompted purchase response. This is to the benefit of shareholders, customers and employees.

Internet

The Internet is a global general public intercommunications network. For a business or organization, the Web site is an Internet site published publicly under an organization's own name. When a select audience only is allowed access through password protection it is called an extranet. An intranet is where the access is limited to employees of the organization's Web site – such a site may be operated entirely internally.

There are estimated to be some 300 million users worldwide. Marketingnet, a leading UK company in Web site consultancy, describe Web sites as achieving one of three types of strategy for business use:

■ presentation – where people can look to gain information;
■ interaction – where people can communicate;
■ representation – where people can transact business (not just financial) without requiring personal intervention.

Marketingnet then look at three ways to offer that marketing strategy:

■ generally available (Internet);
■ available in-house only (intranet);
■ available to a select and targeted exclusive group of people (extranet).

The way you follow the matrix of alternatives is your strategy – the resulting implementations are your marketing activities.

Many firms following a me-too policy put their brochure on a Web site. That is unlikely to do much good. Peter Job CEO of Reuters (December 2000) says 'Online companies specialising purely in content production are doomed.' The key to having successful Internet marketing communications is to 'think through the strategy' – that is, ask how your Web site can help your customers. Think of the 'six Cs'. That should help you decide the purpose of both why you are going on the Web and the context of your Web site – how it fits in with your other marketing activities as seen from the customer view.

There is a need to think through the purpose of a Web site whether you are operating as a business-to-consumer or business-to-business venture. This is the first reason why Web sites fail – often no one thought through the reason for it. In a recent survey (February 2001) only a third of companies responded to an e-mail; nearly half of all companies never responded at all. Tesco with £214 million of orders in 2000, with 750,000 registered users and 60,000 online shoppers each week looks at what its customers are using the site for and make it as easy as possible for them to do it. Seventy per cent of items ordered are fresh, which is surprising. Tesco has 40,000 lines but finds most customers buy only 400 or 500 in a year. Tesco lets customers look at what they bought last time. Domino Pizza has a fast-track repeat of the last order.

The second greatest failure of Web sites to attract customers is the need to maintain and operate them after development. As a yardstick Paul Smith advocates a ratio of resource allocation of 1:2:5 for development: maintenance: operation. This is often the reverse of the ratio applied by inexperienced Web site operators. Setting the example, the BBC changes its Web site daily.

The third failure arises from a failure to integrate the Web site with other marketing activities. The advertisement tempts potential customers to visit a Web site. When they get there they find the home page is quite unrelated to what they were expecting. The Internet site must be a part of a seamless, logical progression for the customer towards making a purchase. Fulfilment of the order is crucial. Many dot.com companies failed because product delivery was so poor. It helps if the product can be delivered by the Royal Mail (fits through a letter box) for the recipient may not be in when the delivery is made. A number of specialists are appearing to assist delivery: Addison Lee (who are also couriers), UPS, M-Box.co.uk (linked with Express Dairies), and I-force.co.uk who use Web site links from client sites to their warehouse and who also process the credit card and deliver.

What can it do?
Paul Smith offers five reasons for having a Web site and an e-mail capability:

■ to help customers get to know you;
■ to get closer to customers;
■ to add value for customers;
■ to build relationships with customers;
■ to save costs (both your own and the customers).

Paul Smith says research shows customers spend more online once a relationship is established. Your Web site should change over a period of time as your business changes and your relationships build. You should plan for the changes when considering the purpose of the Web site itself. You may start with a simple site designed to attract and allow people to proceed to order/buy (research indicates that with the right advertising and some incentive people will visit a Web site once). The site needs to include an incentive for people to return.

You should decide how to strengthen the relationship; whether you are going to offer improvements by offering greater exclusivity to customers through offers of intranets and then extranet membership or move from a simple presentation Web site to one where you offer the customer interaction, then finally allowing the customer a say in the business (representation).

Example of a representation Web site

The site www.Pricerunner.com is an example of a site where comparison of retail outlets for branded products informs the customer of where the product is being sold for the cheapest price. The product can be purchased through links.

The site also allows the customer to input experience of the product post-purchase. The customer can also see other customers' views and what other customers think of other customer reports. This allows a measure of comparison of products in a kind of consumer research report.

The most popular site of this type in the UK is www.shops-mart.com with 466,800 unique visitors in October 2000.

Just as for any other marketing activity, your reasoning for Internet activity should logically follow from your business objectives and the resulting marketing objectives. It should just be one of a range of marketing activities; you will be trying to reach a particular part of the market and hoping to achieve something. And, of course, you must measure it to see that you achieve what you set out to do. You may conclude that the strategy should change over a period of time. To accommodate this you might initially have a 'fun' Web site, offering benefits that then you extend to become an intranet or extranet. You may decide to be involved with a portal.

The production of a Web site can be relatively cheap. Speed of downloading, easy movement between relevant screens, flashing icons are well understood, as are links to other sites, how to be recognized by search engines, and the selection of appropriate meta tags. You do not need to be able to write HTML or XML or design a Web site. In any case, avoid basic Web design packages – they are unlikely to be imaginative enough to make much impact. You do need to understand the limits of the technology – as with all media.

The difficult part of going on the Internet is producing a Web site that people want to revisit – and here the techies cannot help. You need to start with the customers. What do you want them to visit your site for? What will bring them to your site? What will persuade them to stay on your site, persuade them to return and do that many times? How can you build a relationship with the customer? How can you persuade the customer to buy or place an order online?

You need to have thought through the whole process – and from the customer viewpoint. Think of the 'six Cs'. This includes the delivery and fulfilment end. The reason a lot of dot.coms and the associated businesses have failed is that they did not think through how to use the Internet as marketing activity to best effect. Paul Smith argues that as many as 97 per cent of all dot.coms will fail in two years.

*Importance of thinking through the whole process of a
Web site*

Toys'R'Us in the US lost a lot of credibility because they failed
to deliver toys in time for Christmas in 1999. (They also
collected some lawsuits.) Contrast that with Amazon.com who
tell you when the book is due to arrive when you make a
purchase.

In the UK, online bookshops report a fall in trade before
Christmas – the British do not believe books ordered in the
final run-up to Christmas will be delivered on time. Amazon's
service overcomes this perception.

The Internet can also provide a service as part of the overall
concept. In businesses such as carriers delivering parcels and
packets you can watch the progress of an item to its destination
through the Internet. The service is part of the add-on benefit of
having items sent by courier.

How much should it cost? Charlie Dobres believes that no one
should launch anything other than a test site at first. The
maximum expenditure for a month should be £50,000 for a UK plc
– this is no more than a single full-page advertisement in a top
newspaper (as at January 2001). Test marketing – a marketing basic
– should be continued as changes are made. Charlie Dobres
believes that of the £51 million spent in online advertising in 1999
(with 90 per cent on the top 10 publishers' sites) was probably
misused money – the return was probably not measured.

Measuring the achievement is where the techies come in, but
you need to tell them what to measure. Just measuring the number
of hits is really useless, as described earlier. Measuring unique visitors is better but does not mean the site is successful. Counting
visitors who indicate how they found the site is a measure of the
success of some other marketing activity, say an advertisement
that led them there. Where they have come from can indicate
coverage of an advertisement. National newspapers promising
regional coverage can be checked by analysis of the postcode registrations of Web site visitors.

If you do set up a Web site it is as a marketing activity to achieve
part of a marketing objective. Do not lose sight of this.

It is very easy to allow the techies to measure everything – particularly adopting clever ways of measuring. Then you are left with masses of data, none of which may be directly relevant. A number of firms offer software that records where visitors have come from (which country even), which day they visited, which pages were looked at, where they went on to; clearly a key record is 'who are repeat or regular visitors?' There is a need to communicate with those who register. What is the purpose of obtaining registrations if you do not subsequently communicate with them? You need to develop a follow-up programme. Few seem to do so yet the research quoted by Paul Smith indicates that more purchases are made when a relationship has been established.

For example, suppose that the marketing objective is to increase awareness of your products/services to a particular target market. Then you want to measure the number of hits people make on products/services and perhaps their prices on different pages. But visitors to the pages are not enough. You need to know if they are the right people. Are the people visiting your site your target market? You are trying to establish a dialogue – a relationship – so that you can find out if the visitors match your target profile. You want to establish as many facts as you need about them. This helps you to define your target market. An easy way to find this out is to get them to register. You can then, by asking appropriate questions, find out if they do match. If you have not made the site interesting enough or they can perceive little of value to them, they may not bother to register. You may need to have additional information. A postcode can be identified with people of probable target markets. So you could ask for their postcode. People know that postcodes give an address – so they may assume that is the purpose of your question. However not all people are who they seem – some use aliases, some use a number of Web sites or e-mail addresses, some will use deliberately misleading information. Beware.

You may have to offer an incentive that browsers will believe will be of value to them. An example of an incentive is to offer access to closed pages once they have registered – the closed pages being of some perceived value. SkyTV offer prizes for picking sports teams. Others offer games with a highest score to beat. Others offer competitions. You must fulfil the promise. An alternative is to offer a real redeemable incentive. By registering at the

Oddbins Web site you could then enter a page and obtain a voucher that you can print. Presenting the voucher at an Oddbins store allows you to obtain 12.5 per cent off a case of wine. Some offer redeemable book vouchers.

Be aware that some site affiliations reward one advertiser through a roving 'cookie'. It just means that commissions are paid to links along the way for introductions and better still, purchases at the final site.

It is possible to complete detailed questionnaires and give permission to be sent e-mail offers of a particular interest (an example is www.lifeminders.com).

If the object is to sell, clearly then you need to measure sales. You probably want to know who is buying what. If they buy more than once that too may be important. Repeat purchasers need to be encouraged. You may wish to send an email with an offer. In the United States it is customary for businesses to send emails at night or weekends.

An example of Internet use – taxi drivers

You may not think that the Internet is a suitable place to sell a service such as taxi hire. An Ipswich taxi driver obtains many taxi hirings from his Internet listing with search engines. The main users of his taxi service are Americans flying into Stanstead, often to visit US Forces relatives based in the Anglia area. They are accustomed to using the Internet. They search for a taxi to meet their flight. There are few other taxi services offering their trade on the Internet.

Measurement mechanisms
A list of measurement mechanisms has already been raised:

■ How many times do visitors return?
■ What is the route they take around the site?
■ Which parts of the Web site do they visit and for how long?
■ Do they buy and what do they buy?
■ Is the profile of the site visitors the target market you seek to attract?

From this you find what is of interest to each visitor; you are particularly keen to know all about any buyers and of course you should have a series of marketing activities that develop the relationship with them and any registrants. The perception is that few firms do this – the author has registered with many sites but none come back with anything. Why not? Because they do not think through the marketing objective applied to the marketing activity of starting a Web site.

You can track from site entry how people move round the site. The site www.milwardbrown.com offers software products that can measure an Internet site and profile customers; other firms offer measuring products.

By requiring customers to register to enter suitably enticing parts of the site, you can find out who they are and build up a database of names and addresses and email addresses (the Data Protection Act applies).

For each advertisement or banner link, you can send people to a different home page – this will tell you the trigger for them seeing the site. It is also a way to measure advertising achievement, for example. (Note that the effectiveness of banner sites is being questioned and that larger advertising areas may be the norm in future.)

You should measure day of the week, time, what they buy and what parts of the site they visit. This will help in the future when you communicate as part of a customer relationship marketing activity.

A part of the site should allow feedback (e-mails). The frequency of e-mail use should be measured and, of course, the content should be studied.

The cost of the marketing activity – setting up the Web site – should be measured against the target. The contribution to bottom line profit should be measured.

An example of the rise and fall of a dot.com company

Clust.com is the tale of a company that rose to prominence, but after eight months the company died. Each advertisement, particularly when shown in cinemas, saw a flood of people visiting the site. However, the flood quickly faded away and was not sustained – the visitors did not return because the site was not interesting enough. They did not purchase and the delivery side was never thought through. Registration allowed entry to a competition, though only a fifth of the numbers forecast did in fact register. The firm had not thought of what to do with those who had registered. The cost to recruit those who did register was about £10 per head.

It is best to advertise on sites where the recipient has access to pen and paper and far better still has access to the Internet itself to hand. How many times have you seen a Web site in the cinema, advertised on the side of a bus or on the Underground and you forget it or are unable to write it down? It is not easy to record information about transport advertisements, such as Web site addresses, even though the product or service is attractive – most frequently on cost grounds. Even when you are sure of the name, you forget 'was it .com or .co.uk?' Unless you have a brand that is a name – such as easyjet.com – you may be fighting a losing battle.

There are a few real experts in this area of marketing communications. Marketingnet.com is a business that has such expertise. If you are new to the Internet, do take advice or accept training.

Tip

Because of the limitations of web pages – size and shape and colour constraints – if you are starting from scratch, design a Web logo to go on an interactive TV screen Internet Web site first, then translate it into other kinds of media. It will cost you less.

Mobile Internet

What is it?

This is advertising through mobile phones. This medium is in its infancy. It arises out of the amazing take-up – particularly by 18 to 24 year olds – of text messaging. All mobile phones can text message. There are some 40 million phones in the UK. WAP mobile phones can also achieve limited access to the Internet. Later technology will improve the capabilities. It is a global activity. In the UK alone it is reported in that one month that some 766 million messages were sent. It is addictive to those who use it. A cult and language have developed with it. It is fast. It is trendy – people in this age group will not leave home without their mobiles.

People use text messaging because it is fun: 70 per cent use it for humour, 60 per cent use it to make social arrangements. It removes voice contact, which can give people greater confidence in communication. It is a wireless system and is not linked to a fixed line. The text is limited to 160 characters per screen. It is capable of displaying logos or cartoons on screen. Playing games is a feature. It is not a place to surf. Users can download ringing tones (10,000 are doing this each day). These ringing tones can be up to three minutes long. This is equivalent to a pop record.

It is a permission-based lifestyle-centred communication device, which is carried by the person and is often permanently on. A text message is short and usually pithy and uses the developed text language.

What can it do?
You require a telephone number list of an appropriate market segment of customers with all those listed giving approval for their numbers to be used. This approval for listing is often carried out online using Web sites. A firm such as AirMedia can advise on listings and help prepare campaigns of text messages that match the customer acceptance of text messages – such acceptance is researched for both frequency and acceptability of material. The user can limit the information they wish to receive. AirMedia have clients such as Manchester United, MTV, Jennifer Lopez. AirMedia offer four products which cover alerts, special news, behind scenes comment, and m-commerce (used for box office activity – for example Austrian railways allow ticket booking through text messaging).

An example of one list intermediary is Nightfly – a business set up by Diageo, the drinks company. By the time this book is in print there will be some 100,000 under-30 year olds who have signed up to Nightfly. Nightfly covers 11 cities in the UK with 30 channels with which the user can chose to connect. Channels cover nightlife – clubs and bars, events listings, what's on television, hairdressing and beauty, magazines, travel, humour and fashion. Nightfly with its Diageo link is primarily an entertainment operator.

Diageo promotions of its Guinness and Smirnoff brands have included free drinks or two-for-the-price-of-one at certain bars between certain times on certain nights on presentation at the bar of the text message on the mobile phone. These can in future be tied into a reader kept behind the bar. Many promoters however are content to allow much wider broadcasting of offers through viral activity and are happy with the extra trade generated. Nightfly has 10 fields for profile acquisition as part of the registration process and sophisticated monitoring of its customers.

Access to Nightfly channels is free to the user – the sponsor/advertiser pays the cost. Registration is through a call centre, on the Internet or face to face in participating bars themselves. Sony, EMI and some grocery multiples are now taking up the challenge of the mobile Internet with Nightfly.

The opportunities are still being explored but text messaging can be used as a billboard. It can be used as an alert – for example the mobile rings whenever a specified football team scores a goal or when tickets or a CD are put on sale. As a traffic driver, it can magnify take-up of tickets and attendance at events. It is used for competitions to enhance branding. Here it is particularly beneficial as a two-way communicator – typically 40 per cent of users targeted from the customer database respond to competitions benefiting from a reward on completion – a brand product. The communication also allows the passing back of useful quantitative market research information to the operator.

Measuring it

The profile of a customer is typically of around 10 fields, with every text message out and every response in, recorded. Entry in competitions and completion of each stage is recorded. Take-up of rewards is recorded – typically 50 per cent within the first month. Measurement and reporting can be tailored to a firm's needs.

The typical cost of a six-month trial using 5,000 users sending five messages a week is likely to be around £50,000. On this basis text messaging is some three times cheaper per conversion compared with a mailshot or 15 times cheaper than a flyer or the Internet. However, as this book goes to print there are plenty of offers now of £5,000 for 2,500 users for two months with design and other costs waived. Now is the time to test this market – the Appendix has references to providers.

Measurement mechanisms

These need to be discussed with the providers who are effectively pioneering measurement systems. The principle should still apply – obtain measurement against your key performance indicator and metric to ensure that you have value-for-money marketing.

Interactive television

What is it?

Interactive television is a television that has a communication facility. The TV set is coupled to a set-top box that has a communication access through a telephone line.

To be able to operate interactive TV, the TV set must be digital. The BBC plans that within 10 to 15 years all transmissions will be digital – so many sets will need to be converted or discarded. At present (January 2001) there are 5.7 million digital TV households in the UK. Sky TV, with 4.2 million, has interactive TV on 12 of its channels; NTL (about half a million) and ONDigital will be interactive shortly. BT is to introduce ADSL (Assymetric Digital Strap Line) (Homechoice in the Hammersmith area is a trial). Digital Sky TV users have free access to Open… which is the interactive channel (Open… is a commercial name). Though Open… is 'platform neutral' its ownership is 80 per cent SkyTV.

For Sky, to access and operate the interactivity merely requires handling the familiar remote control box, with a modification of four additional buttons. The button colour and placing is reproduced on screen and options to press are highlighted on screen. The set-top box has two smart cards, which retain information such as favourite channels and credit card numbers.

When viewers watch an interactive advertisement on Sky TV (a 'pop up' on the TV screen offers the option to interact) and if they decide to go interactive they press a button matching the 'pop up' to interact and are then switched across to the Open… channel and a branded location. Here they follow instructions for more information or maybe make a request to be sent a brochure or progress to make a purchase. Open… describe soft use as using e-mail, obtaining more information or sending for the brochure. Hard use is when a purchase is made. About 10 per cent of Sky TV subscribers have made a purchase.

Interactive TV is set to become the greatest marketing communication activity ever – even greater than the Internet. The system has been operating and growing for a year in the UK. Already the Open… channel claims it is the third largest e-mail provider (December 2000). Paul Cheesbrough of the BBC (in December 2000) says that 25 per cent of UK households now have digital TV (compared to 8 per cent in Europe) with PC and digital TV penetration estimated to be about equal in 2003. Forrester Research forecast that by 2005 more Europeans will be using interactive TV than going online to use the Internet.

Interactive TV has many advantages over the Internet. It is described as a 'lean back' medium. It is accepted as part of the family. A television set is trusted in the home. It lives in the living room and is often surrounded by the family who all frequently watch it together, whereas the computer is in another room, usually with only a single person in front of it. Interactive TV is put across as allowing people to go out from their homes to obtain information or purchase without leaving their homes – it is not promoted as intrusive in any way.

Interactive TV uses telephone line access less than the Internet. The access is at the local or free call rate. Complex graphics and pictures are sent through the transmission signal. One disadvantage of interactive TV is that it is typically viewed at a distance of three metres compared with a PC when viewing the Internet at half a metre. This means that lettering and words and the effective written message area is much reduced – alternatively many screens have to be viewed. The logical process for a customer must be followed, if using many screens. There will be resistance to too many screens in any case.

The perceived and actual security is greater than the Internet. Security comes from the fact the database holds details of the address and telephone number of the customer and the set-top box has its own unique security code. The set-top box is also installed – that is connection is made to a specific telephone line, say by a Sky or NTL TV technician who confirms the address and telephone line number associated with the box. This means that it is not possible to steal and use a box elsewhere. The same applies to a credit card; using a wrong/stolen credit card causes a security alert when the check is made before purchase is sanctioned and the purchase can be rejected, the police informed and so forth.

Actually using interactive TV, Open... offers a number of alternatives. Sky TV currently only allows the last advertisement in a commercial break to be interactive and it has to be 30 seconds long. This means that it is expensive, although cheaper than an ITV advertisement, but note that Sky 1 is not far behind ITV. The price varies as to which Sky channel is used. Open... are also offering shopping mall opportunities – similar to a concession in a department store – where a number of advertisers can combine to use one 30-second slot on Sky TV and then this is expanded on the open channel as viewers switch to interactive. The offer makes use of Open Xtra with fulfilment (delivery) as one delivery charge. It has been shown that many dot.com companies failed because they could not deliver – they had not thought through the management of the whole operation. Open... is trying to overcome this – and maintain their reputation.

The technical support available from Open... to set up an interactive TV advertisement includes the use of templates that conform to the preferred operation of the remote control and what is shown and where it is on screen. In effect the screen size is less than on the Internet to make it user friendly. There is scope to include a jump to a complete Web site equivalent (Open... does not advocate putting a standard Web page on the TV screen, preferring a cut-down page for easier viewing).

What can it do?
The commercial links between Sky TV and Open... now mean that the two databases can be combined. Sky TV know who their subscribers are – from a profile drawn up at installation, although information about who is watching what still has to be obtained through audience research at any time. The databases will be capable of storing the channel and viewing preferences of the subscriber. The situation changes the moment the subscriber switches to Open...

The Open... database tracks interactivity and purchases. Clearly specific channel purchase will identify purchaser and buying interests from billing details. It will be possible to data mine, giving an ability to target at a later date. The smart card capacity in the set-top box will allow some 100 loyalty cards. Open... will also allow shortly a 'store and forward' facility allowing a customer to earmark an interest in a product without disturbing the watching, of a programme. Interactive screens will also allow the product to be shown in colour variants. A 'jump to' facility will offer extras such as 'call me'; that is giving permission to be telephoned. Transactions can take place, while still watching, once details of credit cards are entered on a smart card in the set-top box. A 'Call polling' facility, if enabled, will allow access to customer data. Retailers will be able to offer discounts online in real time.

The commercial situation, after one year (as at November 2000), is that interactive TV is being used to purchase in order of popularity: pizzas, mobile phones, CDs and DVDs. Woolworths find that even selling only 275 entertainment products (normally nearer 15,000 product lines are found in the average store) the interactive TV sales are equivalent to a store in 173rd place of their 800 outlets. Mobile phone sales are equal to two flagship stores in Oxford Street. A high street bank (HSBC) finds its interactive sales activity equivalent to 12 medium-sized banks. And people buy at all times not just during the day. One product launch promotion secured 3,000 orders in three hours between 4 am and 7 am.

TV producers have yet to consider how they could enhance their productions adding in-depth programme material. This could include advertisements. In the near future it will be possible to interact during programmes and offer people the choice of products including clothes being worn and used by actors; 'as seen on TV', showing products on a TV programme will be in real time. Playing TV game show games is another huge growth area presently under research; the potential for advertisers with universal game show participation is still being explored. Open... have trialled a Trivial Pursuit game five times and obtained 1.6 million entries using a prime-time telephone number which has proved to be a substantial revenue generator.

A limitation to growth of interactive TV may be the use of TIVO sets which have the storage capacity to allow purchasers of the TIVO set-top box to remove advertisements; however this is offset by the ability of viewers to purchase products through 'as-seen-on-TV' promotions in parallel with programmes through the 'pop up' facility. The industry expect a hard core of 5 per cent of subscribers will resist seeing advertisements on TV using TIVO.

Paul Cheesbrough advocates careful selection of the platform with which to go interactive, a view supported by Charlie Dobres. Open... is not actually an open channel. Each channel operates with different systems; there is no standard. This adds to cost if more than one platform is proposed, as the same material for inter-active TV has to be reprocessed. It is not possible to create the material once and publish it everywhere. Each platform has quite different demographics. Middle England does now subscribe. The over-50 age group and the disabled make great use of interactive TV.

It is normally recommended for any TV advertisement that an alternative response mechanism is given, such as a Web site address or a call centre telephone number or both.

Measuring achievement

If you decide on interactive TV as a marketing activity, you need to be clear as to why you have selected it and this will point to what you need to measure. Interactive TV is probably at present most suited as a business-to-consumer marketing activity because watching television in the office is probably unacceptable within the existing business culture. As for all marketing communications you need to check that your target market is or is likely to be soon a confirmed user of interactive TV and that you put across your message to match the customer need. And you then measure the achievement.

You probably need to know that you are reaching your target market. You can only rely on BARB (Broadcasters Audience Research Board) TV viewing figures until the viewer goes interac-tive. Once interactive use is selected, you can rapidly confirm through a mix of any registration questions, the set-top box and the subscriber details, who has gone interactive. You need, of course, to have a profile of your existing customers as a preferred target market. You can track the person not only for the number of visits to a site, but their route around the site. Did they order a brochure and then after they received it did they visit the site again? How long do they stay on any visit and finally when was the order or purchase made?

Clearly eventual success is an order for purchase. Again it is possible to track how many times a person goes interactive and visits the site before making the purchase. This will indicate how many times an advertisement needs to be shown. Tracking will also indicate which advertisement and when it was shown, which will help future slot purchase. Did the person go interactive immediately on seeing the advertisement? Did the person wait? For how long?

You probably need to know whether you are using the best commercial. This is one medium where the mechanisms for measuring response in real time allow you to tweak the advertisements and information you supply on the open channel. If one advertisement triggers a poor response it can be pulled and one that attracts a more favourable response can be used instead.

If viewers are going interactive but not ordering or buying, you can change the offer. Almost in real time.

The expertise of the interactive TV provider is important here but it does not mean that you should abrogate responsibility for defining the marketing measurement objectives that interactive TV is to achieve for you.

Achievement mechanisms

You can only record advertisement viewing audiences using the BARB figure as for any TV viewing.

The situation changes the moment a viewer presses the interactive button. This indicates an interest in the product or service – which can be recorded. It is possible to track a viewer through screens and the buttons pressed and in which order. The system will also record any soft activity such as sending for brochures or more information or hard activity such as making purchases. This means that the effectiveness of a site can be fully recorded. The effectiveness of the commercial causing viewers to go interactive can be measured.

At this early stage of interactive TV development it is best to take advice from Open... As for all marketing communications you need to check that your target market is or is likely to be soon a confirmed user of interactive TV and that you put across your message to match the customer need. And you then measure the achievement.

The alternative response mechanisms given, such as a Web site address or call centre telephone number or both, need to be primed as usual to ask where the caller saw the TV advertisement. The Web site design can include a response to record where the Web site address was seen if the potential customer is not coming into the Web site directly from interactive TV. Should a viewer transfer to the Internet while on TV then the normal measurement mechanisms of an Internet site apply – see above.

It is possible to record overall the customer preference for response and the route towards that. This is useful for future campaign design and marketing activity selection. The allocation of resource to a call centre might not be required if few select that means of responding.

5

Direct marketing communications

For an understanding and feel for direct marketing the fourth edition of Drayton Bird's *Commonsense Direct Marketing* is a lovely, readable book and he describes direct marketing as 'an advertising activity which creates and exploits a direct relationship between you and your prospect or customer as an individual'. Direct marketing is comfortable with complex propositions. It must be applied intelligently and the database properly used.

Good copy can draw attention, build conviction and draw on the power of emotion. Testing copy is essential but Drayton Bird implies that it is not always done – he believes in the maxim that you should not change copy until you have found something better. He considers there are five major activities that can be applied singly or in stages or over time developing a relationship for direct marketing to persuade the recipient to:

- buy through the post;
- ask for catalogues;
- request a demonstration;
- visit a retail establishment;
- take part in some action.

Judith Donovan's book *DIY Direct Marketing* describes itself 'as an essential guide for beginners'. It is just what it says on the cover.

Her definition of Direct marketing is that it is 'the science of arresting the human intelligence long enough to take money off it'. She describes each of the activities given below well and includes useful tips. The start point she insists must be a series of questions:

Question	Answer
Who am I trying to reach?	A specific target; that is what direct mail is good at.
What do I want them to do?	See Drayton Bird's list above.
Why should they do it?	Give clear 'six Cs' customer benefits
Where should I reach them?	The area – are you tying in the direct mail with TV ads, say?
When should I reach them?	Midweek for business, weekend for consumers.

Judith Donovan also advocates that key database information items for each customer are recency, frequency, value and product. The response to direct marketing can be enhanced with a truly exclusive offer – treatment like a VIP, requiring a rapid response, the offer of a gift that is out of the ordinary. Read her practical book – she's worth it.

Direct mail

What is it?
Direct mail is 'writing an offer that is creatively presented sending it out on a good list usually via Royal Mail with some form of response mechanism – not forgetting the envelope'. Judith Donovan's book contains plenty of advice on list purchase, creative consideration and envelopes. She stresses the feel must be right – direct mail is a tactile medium.

What can it do?
It is the subject of much market research and is difficult to prove – some say that 62 per cent is thrown away, while 22 per cent is read carefully, with 16 per cent glanced at. Typical target response rates are less than one per cent. A typical cost of the mailshot itself is 50 pence per recipient (December 2000). You may have to wait for reorders to recoup the costs.

Direct mail may well be one of several associated marketing activities forming a campaign. A campaign may consist of some advertisements in an area followed by a direct mailshot in the same area followed by telemarketing with two follow-up mailings to those who do not respond initially. This sort of approach works, for example, for buying cases of better-than-average wine (more highly priced wine) to people who are likely to drink wine regularly and are likely to have the appropriate income (and probably live in an upmarket area).

Direct mail is certainly suited to products or services that do not need to be sampled (wine is not normally sampled prior to purchase), need to be worn to determine fit (mail order rather than direct mail covers clothing sales where detailed measurements are entered into the order form), or require a degree of consideration of a complex proposition (financial services offers).

Measuring achievement

If the objective for which this marketing activity is implemented is, say, to find new regular customers, those who will come back to buy again and again, you would probably want to measure long-term value, say over two years or as an alternative, measure the profile of those responding to confirm that their profile matches the existing customer profile. If you measure short-term value – straight orders taken against the cost of the direct mailing – then you may not find it a cost-effective marketing activity.

You should probably expect a return of less than 1 per cent for a direct mailing. The profit margin of the resulting single orders placed will probably not cover the cost of the direct mailing. But if your new customers are the same profile as your existing regular customers then you have a high probability that they will reorder.

It is worth noting that if:

▪ you do not direct mail to sufficient numbers; or
▪ you mis-target your mailshot; or
▪ you did not test the copy;
▪ then this marketing activity would probably fail whatever measure you use.

The failure might stem from the original setting of the business objective and not ascertaining whether the objective is SMART.

The marketing objective that followed should lead to buying a list that matched the existing profile of your customers which assumes you knew that profile. If you did not know the profile you should set that as a marketing activity before you purchase a list. You might measure that profiling success by taking a sample, checking their views through market research. You should also test the copy – that could be done alongside the market research. You will only discover whether your offer has been understood through market research.

Direct mail - example of calculating the return

Say you have 400 regular customers and you set as a business objective a growth target of 10 per cent – you want another 40 customers. Assuming you then apply the SMART criteria on the objective (see Chapter 2), the marketing objective is to communicate an offer to a sufficient number of an appropriate target market that they become customers. Then, say, on a mailing of 100,000 at 50 pence per mail-out, you get a 0.3 per cent response and that will produce 300 enquiries. Cost per enquiry is £167. If the enquiries result in 150 sales then the cost per sale is £333. Depending on your margin for just 150 sales this is unlikely to cover the cost. But if the 150 reorder – that is buy again and again – eventually the margin on their sales will cover the direct mail marketing activity.

The single measure of recording how many out of the 100,000 made a purchase is unsafe in that you will certainly be open to accusations of straightforward bottom-line failure. A better measure is to see whether you have got any new customers of your preferred type – your target market. You need to have already recorded, or put in hand marketing activity to record now, the characteristics/profiles of your regular customers including their purchasing behaviour. You now measure the characteristics/profiles of the new customers that made the 150 sales. If they are of a similar profile to your existing customers then you could probably expect that you have achieved the aim several times over (3.75 times in fact). If all 150 match – well done! You would still find that you achieve your aim of at least 40 new customers even if two-thirds are only single-time purchasers. That would leave 50 new customers. You might, through additional marketing activity, cajole some of the 100 who made one purchase back.

If your measure of success is just sales, in one year you will not record success. Rather, measure profile match.

Achievement mechanisms

- Measure new customer sales, repeat sales, order values.
- Measure cost per inquiry, cost per sale, numbers of new customers
- Measure characteristic/profile of existing regular customers and characteristic/profile of new customers. Confirm a match.
- Measure cost of marketing activity versus target. The effect on profit – but over a long time for positive results.

E-mail

What is it?
An e-mail is an Internet-related communication. It is sent to an e-mail addressee. It is possible to set up a mailing list, which will both address and personalize e-mails in bulk. This can be achieved through the Internet.

What it can do
It is useful for keeping in touch with existing customers. You need an e-mail database. If you have collected e-mails from existing customers then these can form a very useful database for marketing purposes.

E-mails can offer routine information that customers like from their suppliers. You should make your e-mails of value to customers and worth viewing; to achieve this it is of benefit to include hidden offers – that is make one-off offers within the e-mail itself or include invitations or other benefits.

Information about new product launches should again be provided alongside an offer to make reading your e-mails an exciting purposeful process.

You may also set an alert and automatic e-mail response to potential customers registering at your site. The alert could prompt a salesperson to make a telephone call.

Note that the Data Protection Act covers databases. (See Appendix 1 for addresses/Web sites.)

Measuring achievement
The purpose of the e-mails should help decide what measurements to make for successful achievement.

If it is a means to boost sales then you would need to know the present sales of existing customers and measure the result after sending out the e-mails.

You may find that just using e-mails to keep customers informed about existing products and prices achieves little – again this could be measured. Perhaps the use of an incentive would help – a sale or discount perhaps only to specified customers or the first 20 to respond. Measure the result. Again customers are busy persons and may not respond to too-frequent contact. Customers should be asked how often they prefer to be contacted – see Chapter 2.

If the purpose for which this e-mail marketing activity is implemented is awareness then some form of questionnaire – which could be Internet based – would measure how successfully customers' knowledge is kept up to date. An Internet-based response questionnaire is available from the suppliers of the CD ROM issued with this book.

Achievement mechanisms
Measure sales of existing products to regular customers and compare with previous period, measure sales of new products to existing customers. Measure any changes of sales after sending out any e-mail. Track purchase value and size of orders.

Measure cost of marketing activity versus target. The cost of sending out e-mails is small, especially if done in bulk. Measure the effect on profit.

As a check on awareness it might be worth e-mailing a questionnaire as a customer survey including questions to ascertain their knowledge of products and prices. Questionnaires can be constructed using the SNAP software and automated through the SNAP survey software – see the free CD ROM included with this book.

Questionnaires can be Internet based. Mercator provide such software as additional to their basic product.

Telemarketing

What is it?

A person or team of persons calling potential customers from a list. It can be used for anything. Judith Donovan recommends it for:

- following up mailshots of expensive products;
- taking orders;
- validating lists;
- keeping in touch with marginal accounts;
- arranging meetings and appointments;
- customer communication (for example – 'there's a sale on now').

Telemarketing is an outgoing task for a call centre.

What can it do?

Contact can be made with many people in a day (depends on the size of the team), the contact is flexible and live, it allows two-way communication. It has no geographic restrictions. It allows cross-selling and upselling. Orders can be taken on the spot. It is not popular with consumers when used as a cold calling. It is understood by business customers as a method of entry. In Helmsmen's experience it is best used with some 'link' – that is a link should make the call 'offer' relevant and clearly beneficial to the business recipient. It is not visual and therefore is best used to sell services or after a service/product mailshot.

You always need to agree a script which gives 'pointers to the operator' – usually in a tree/branch format, which follows likely potential responses from the customer.

Time should be spent agreeing a script. The final script should be tested both to see if the call centre person is happy using it and to see if the recipient understands it. The agreed script for the call should not only ascertain that the correct person on the list is called but should have questions that confirm that they match the profile as described by the list broker presumably matching your customer profile. The main purpose is then to put the proposition – the reason for the call. The 'link' should precede the action to which you want the caller to agree to if you are arranging meetings or appointments.

Using telemarketing (a call centre for outgoing calls) is a better way of obtaining a response from a customer than asking a customer to send a letter back from a mail order mailshot, direct response TV, an advertisement, or even an Internet Web site. A call centre operator can obtain much more information and clear up misunderstandings. They can get a feel for slight variations in meaning that may be significant.

A telemarketing person using a questionnaire can typically make around six useful calls an hour at most – even with auto-mated dialling. This call rate allows for failed calls, calls back later and the respondents being absent on holiday, sick and so forth. Be aware that calls should only be made at appropriate times of the day. Most people are busy on a Monday while on Friday they may be thinking of other things. Match the call times to the best time of your target's availability and when they are likely to be most receptive. When setting up the work you should build a test period into the contract. Stop after a few hours to find out the experience of the telemarketing team. Certain parts of the script may be diffi-cult to put across or misunderstood or unnecessary. The team will tell you what to cut and where to expand. Make the adjustments. They also keep a log and this can confirm the appropriateness of days/times to call.

Measuring achievement

The purpose of the telemarketing activity will define to an extent what you want to be measured. For sales or fixing appointments the bottom line is probably your ultimate achievement criteria here. Record how many people bought as a result, or accepted an appointment, or the number with whom you are keeping in contact who were converted to ordinary rather than marginal customers.

For appointments you might expect a 1-in-10 success rate (300 calls giving 30 appointments).

The rate of conversions of the appointments subsequently into actual work and the value of that work should be measured. Measure cost of marketing activity versus target. Measure the effect on profit.

The validity of the list is another item to measure in any case. You may discover whether you are calling the right kind of people by examining responses to the questionnaire. Typically any list will be 10 per cent out of date. More than this and you should be unhappy with the list broker.

Achievement mechanisms

A record of each call is held. The parameters of the record can be varied with experience; when the task is set up the subtle alternatives are not always readily apparent. A check on the validity of data may be needed. Some data can be confirmed from other sources and will simplify the task of recording. For example, software is available that lists all UK addresses, once a postcode is obtained, so a call centre operator can save time and confirm residency. The software works alongside the call taker. Each UK postcode covers just a few addresses.

Response by area is readily obtained as is response in time and date blocks. Operators enter the answers to questions into the relevant sections of the database at the time. It is easy then to obtain feedback on response rates/percentages, etc.

The work of the telemarketers themselves can be assessed – using test calls (a competent firm will be routinely testing anyway). The log should be available to you and the work rate should be readily apparent. The log will also show the most successful times of the day and the difficulty of obtaining some persons.

You may wish to set up in-house tracking measures of the subsequent benefit of the telemarketing marketing activity.

Direct response advertisement (magazines and TV)

What is it?

Judith Donovan gives excellent advice on advertising in a magazine and the use of the coupon; she says choosing the right magazine is crucial and tells you how to use BRAD (British Rate and Data), NRS (National Readership Survey) and TGI (Target Group Index) to achieve this. The use of 'tip-ons', a response card stuck on the advertisement, is reputed to be much more effective than a coupon or an insert.

A direct response advertisement is best for complex products and services that require more literature to explain them, or where a demonstration or video or CD ROM is required.

Direct response TV needs clear telephone numbers and a large call centre operation to take calls in breaks. The use of a call centre is covered in a later section. It is the pre-runner to interactive TV. Research shows that on average people watch around 90 hours of a shopping channel before making a purchase.

Further marketing activities should be planned to take up the response. A 'fulfilment' mailshot is probably the minimum. Fulfilment means carrying out the agreed offer: this may be sending out the brochure offered and requested in the response. Follow-up calls or mailings should be considered whether an order is placed or not to try again to convert the expression of interest to a sales order or to find out why no further action has been taken. To confirm that the respondents match your customer profile you may need to send a questionnaire – the questionnaire could be covered in part on the coupon.

Response to a direct response advertisement can be enhanced with the use of an incentive – it may just be a promotional video or CD ROM, which contains other material likely to be of interest to the potential customer. A gift of some kind may be offered if the coupon is returned. A brochure is the basic response.

What can it do?

It can allow a person, on impulse, to request to be sent more information about the concept – product or service – on offer. It might be a product sample in addition to the information. It is probably unlikely to achieve more than that.

The use of the 'tip-on' with prepaid postage means that people do not have to find an envelope, or copy an address, or find a stamp (assuming it is a prepaid card).

Direct response advertising will require other marketing activities in support; for TV, a call centre is probably the easiest marketing activity to use, for a mailed response a fulfilment operation. There are fulfilment service houses that will do this work.

Measuring achievement

A simple printed code can be used on the coupon and all returns recorded against that advertisement. Follow-up by a call centre is covered under the call centre section. A fulfilment house will record and collate all the coupon or questionnaire information, by date if you require it.

Achievement may be a predetermined percentage response to the advertisement. But the real achievement is how many become customers in the longer term. A tracking system will be required to follow the stages leading up to an order being placed. Initial orders placed may be insufficient to cover the cost of the marketing activities. The aim must be to build up long-term customers – which leads back nicely to the careful selection of the magazine or TV programme, which is the key to success. It also presumes you have a profile of your customers so you know whether you have acquired more of the right type. Market research will indicate the magazine or programme alongside which to place your advertisement that your target market reads or views. Market research will provide you with a customer profile.

Achievement mechanisms

A system of recording responses to the advertisement as a separate entity is required. It might be helpful to record by postcode and date as well. This will confirm the reach of the magazine or TV channel and that the advertisers have delivered.

It will be useful to have buyers across the area to sample and confirm that the 'tip-ons' are affixed. Further information can be obtained about the effectiveness of the advertisements by questioning or sending out questionnaires to those that did respond as to their reasons for doing so and to assess whether they match the target customer profile.

Confirmation about new customers being of the right type requires their profile to be matched with existing customer profiles.

Measure cost of marketing activity versus target. The effect is on profit but over a period of time.

Door-to door

What is it?
Delivery by hand either through the Royal Mail alongside the normal post (Judith Donovan's tip is to use a normal envelope but create an overprint on it of a fake franking to make it seem like

mail) or through a number of organizations that do door-to-door delivery. As you will not be addressing the envelope to an individual you need some form of salutation that is upbeat. For blanket covering an area of high-density housing it can be a cost-effective method of direct communication. It does not require the expense of purchasing lists. It can be used in appropriate areas for local services ranging from those of an estate agent (typically a free valuation) or a solicitor (free short initial consultation) to an offer of a haircut.

Typically a door-to-door should seek a response that gives an opportunity to acquire a name and address from those who take up the offer made. It may well be just one of a number of marketing activities planned with follow-up marketing activities using the names and addresses acquired from respondents to send out mailshots.

What can it do?
It can be the cheapest method of delivering your message or offer. It gives blanket cover of an area. It does not discriminate. It is a way of delivering product samples with a money-off voucher for a follow-up purchase.

The voucher or coupon might ask for a name and address at minimum. It is useful for piloting or testing a new product launch. It practically introduces potential customers to the product or invites them to try a service. Your staff should be trained to expect the response and know how to handle it. It is the start of customer relations with a potential long-term customer – the opportunity should not be thrown away. How often do you use a coupon and give your name and address for a meal/takeaway offer or meal delivery? Then you never hear anything again. If there had been a follow-up a bond might have formed. Regular customers could be rewarded by further vouchers. Viking, the office suppliers, are excellent at following up, with personalized offers in subsequent mailshots.

Any follow-up marketing activity, a real mailing to those responding or a telemarketing call may further enhance sales but the results should be measured.

Measuring achievement
The number of voucher-accompanied purchases can indicate that

the distribution was made and that customers understood, believed and valued the offer sufficiently to make a purchase. Repeat purchase measurement would establish real success.

It may be wise to confirm from some addresses in the targeted area that the material has been delivered. Also check that there are no piles of material sitting in heaps on street corners.

Successful achievement is an increase in sales activity in the outlets to which the customer was directed. The level of success achievement may include a measurement of ongoing repeat sales, as a result of customer bonding to your concept (product or service). This will almost certainly require further marketing activity as a follow-up. The response to these too should be measured.

Achievement mechanisms

Return of the redeemed vouchers from retail outlets can supply information about the purchasers' addresses for further marketing activity. A surge in product or service purchases or enquiries or from increased orders placed by retailers should confirm the success or at least greater interest in the product or service.

Measure orders placed over a period of time from before the door-to-door drop was made. Measure the percentage of vouchers redeemed.

Use CACI research material for the area to compare your take-up by that area and with your customer profile. It might allow more careful door-to-door targeting in any future marketing activity.

Measure cost of marketing activity versus target. Measure the effect on profit.

Catalogue

What is it?

A catalogue of sometimes up to 800 pages is sent out by a mail order firm or delivered by hand by local agents of the firm. Customers can then pick and choose products at leisure, ordering them through the agent or by post or by telephone or by fax or, less usually, by e-mail on the Internet. There is a range of consumer catalogues. Business catalogues also exist. Perhaps Viking are one of the most successful catalogue firms for office products. Five per cent of all retail sales in the UK in 2000 were from catalogues. This is forecast to grow to 9 per cent by 2005 according to Gartner.

Electronic catalogues are available on the Internet. An initial download of the basic catalogue is made. When customers open up the Web site then additional information and prices are added to the basic catalogue. Orders and payment are made electronically.

Catalogues are now produced electronically for business customers in CD ROM format as well as on the Internet. A number of firms offer help with Internet catalogues. There are plenty of examples such as Dell and catalogues of catalogues that compare prices such as Pricerunner. See the Internet section in this chapter.

What can it do?
It allows customers to study products at their leisure. Well-known brands sell well. In business, when an urgent need occurs for a particular part or product, it can be identified from a catalogue before the call is made and the part ordered and paid for and/or delivery arranged. For consumers the ordered items may well be centrally delivered to the agent who then delivers them to consumers at their convenience.

Catalogue selling is often accompanied by offers to encourage purchases and extending the range to friends and relatives of the consumer. Regular customers could be rewarded by further vouchers. Viking obtain repeat orders and develop brand bonding and follows up with personalized offers in subsequent catalogue mailings.

Finance deals are sometimes used to encourage purchases, with extended credit to assist with more order placing. The key is to start a habit of buying from the catalogue, therefore the product and service must be excellent and special offers are needed to encourage early buying.

Judith Donovan believes it is easy to get the format of a catalogue wrong. Hard data from experience indicates the importance of how to set out a catalogue to optimize sales. Research has shown how the eye of the customer moves around a page and how a customer goes through the catalogue. The right mix of photographs, product copy and selling copy are vital. Catalogue design is clearly a specialist task. Use a specialist.

Measuring achievement

The bottom line is clearly the number of sales orders placed or credit sales and/or the interest generated as an income stream. Setting a target of the number of new customers the marketing activity is expected to garner is probably the best challenge. This should be based on the number of potential targets in the area to be targeted. Measure customer retention.

However, as implied in the previous paragraph, there is a need to analyse the placing of products in the catalogue and the pattern of purchasing that results from changes in layout as well as the actual sales. This is the province of the specialist.

The process to achieve regular customers may take time and, when set against actual cost of the marketing activities, in the short term may show a loss. The use of agents calling on consumers operating on a commission-only basis may offset this, removing some of the complexity of delivery and administration by effectively centralizing into one local distributor. The agent is the salesperson and merchandiser and develops customer relations.

The value of actual orders should be measured and set against the cost of the catalogue, delivery and administration.

Achievement mechanisms

You are trying to achieve regular and valuable customers. Measure actual increase and percentage increase in numbers of customers. Record over time whether new customers achieve regular and valuable customer status. Measure customer retention, the effect of sales on product placement within the catalogue, cost of marketing activity versus target, and the effect on profit.

Piggyback

What is it?

It is just what it says, an item of literature included 'piggyback' with a local authority letter or a gas, water, electricity or telephone bill. It is the inclusion of your literature with someone else's mailing. Typically it might be a reply card within a utilities/local authority letter or bill. The card or voucher may be to enable potential customers to place an order or to request a brochure.

What can it do?
It is probably a cheaper alternative than a direct mailing. It can add value to the mailshot it accompanies, for example, an electric power shower leaflet or response card sent out with an electricity or water bill – often with some incentive such as a cost reduction or installation cost reduction. For a one-off purchase of, say, a shower unit, repeat purchases are less likely. For a service or where repeat purchases are required – water filters for example – then it is worth pursuing those that respond initially but subsequently decline, so a brochure offer to obtain names and addresses rather than seeking sales orders may be preferable.

Servicing offers are another example where a piggyback is useful – annual servicing and maintenance of your gas boiler with a gas bill. A piggyback can deliver a message to a particular utility user – specifically targeting a customer. For a service – a maintenance or repair contractor say – then you are looking for long-term customers and it may be an idea to follow up those that responded but did not subsequently take up the order. Those that do take the offer will be sent reminders just before the anniversary.

Piggyback is more precisely targeted than door-to-door or direct mailing to a list. A gas maintenance and service provider would not waste a mailing to a non-gas user; a piggyback offer to a BT user is better than a general mail-out when a BT associated offer is not much help to a customer solely using an NTL cable line.

Piggyback is often successful because of the greater precision of targeting and the carrier's brand providing a status and quality provenance.

Measuring the achievement
Achievement may be a predetermined percentage response to the piggyback, although this is probably only relevant when a brochure is requested as an interim measurement of the success of the message. The value of orders placed is of greater interest. You would no doubt hope that it would be greater than the cost of any piggyback marketing activity.

A fulfilment house will record and collate all the coupon or questionnaire information, by date if you require it. You can set up a similar operation in-house.

If you are carrying out more than one piggyback mailing use a unique code on the particular response voucher to be quoted by the customer when calling or picked up by the fulfilment service to find out which particular piggyback was more or less successful than any other. This may determine which month it is best to send out piggyback mailings – is the poorest response in bleak January or, in fact, do New Year's resolutions hold sway, say, for a gas boiler maintenance contract?

Achievement mechanisms

Measure the response at the point of fulfilment of a sales order or brochure request in terms of numbers and value of any sales orders placed. Collect names and addresses. Measure subsequent marketing activity responses, repeat purchases of products or services – this establishes real success. Measure the cost of marketing activity versus target, and the effect on profit.

Leaflets, handouts

What are they?

It is the placing of leaflets directly into the hands of the potential customer, with persons handing out literature where there is a high footfall of potential customers or self-collection from dispensers at outlets where the customer is likely to pass – widely used in the travel and tourist trade in hotels near the reception/entry hall area.

At exhibitions leaflets can be handed out near the entrance – but check with the organisers – or placed within the carrier bag supplied at registration or entry. Why not consider supplying the carrier bags?

What can they do?

It can draw attention to:

■ a new outlet or new attraction;
■ an existing attraction;
■ a new product or service;
■ a product or service with a limited availability;
■ to a specific exhibition stand.

The leaflet needs to be thought out carefully and the purpose thought through. The leaflet may offer an incentive to encourage a visit or patronage. For an attraction it needs to clearly spell out what is on offer. Distribution is important to consider – it is easy to leave this to chance but unwise.

Leaflet message importance and coverage

On the Swanage Railway on the Isle of Purbeck in Dorset, people assumed that no food was available on the trains and made other arrangements because the leaflet only indicated in small letters on the timetable that a buffet car was available on trains. This misperception was discovered using market research.

The leaflet now spells out food availability – on the train and in station buffets. In consequence the refreshment takings on the railway are now a significant contributor to revenue.

The Swanage Railway market research found people were travelling daily from as far afield as Nottingham to visit the attraction. Leaflet placings previously had been based on the assumption that day trippers would travel no further than from the M4 corridor

---

A leaflet at an exhibition can be used to build a database with space available to enter name, address, and so forth, if it is to be used as a voucher, for say, subscriptions to trade magazines or for an offer of a demonstration at a site away from the exhibition. Subsequent marketing activity can then be applied to achieve sales.

A handout at an exhibition can be used to attract people to a stand offering a prize draw. There is no need for such a handout to ask for names and addresses. To obtain names and addresses of those visiting an exhibition stand it is common practice to call for business cards to be placed in a receptacle with the incentive of an entry into a daily prize draw. Bar code readers of the name tag can achieve the same.

Hotels, information centres and attractions often have their own leaflet dispensers and your leaflet should match the size of the dispenser. In a retail outlet a dispenser may need to be provided – these should be heavily customized – or do not be surprised to find other leaflets placed in true 'cuckoo' fashion. Supplies of leaflet refills and restocking arrangements need to be made, particularly when the leaflet details go out of date.

Measuring achievement

The purpose of the leaflet will govern the achievement measurement. For leaflets used for awareness that are taken from dispensers, staff at an attraction need to be trained to ask how people heard about the attraction and, if through a leaflet, where this was picked up. They could fill in a simple form with the response. This will measure the effectiveness of leaflet distribution as a marketing activity in promoting purchases. It is made easier when the potential customer redeems the leaflet offer – this prompts the staff to start the recording process.

It will be easy to measure the numbers of leaflets handed out by people by recording how many boxes/part-boxes of leaflets they use. If the leaflet includes an incentive then the redemption process can be used to extract information from the customer.

If the leaflet is designed to persuade people just to have a look, note new premises or a retail outlet where you only want to increase awareness, visitors may be counted entering using a number counter (hand operated or electronic). But the opportunity should not be missed to improve bonding and start a customer relationship, hopefully of future repeat business – so the idea of recording names and addresses for a future marketing activity should not be dismissed lightly.

You need to record attendance before the leaflet was offered to track any change. Some form of yardstick may be needed to measure its impact .

You may need to carry out market research into the perceptions and attitudes generated by the leaflet.

Achievement mechanisms

Staff need to be trained in how to respond to a leaflet. At an attraction staff need training in how to ask how people heard about the attraction and how to enter a form with the responses.

Collection of redeemed vouchers and their analysis needs to organized. The distribution of leaflets and quantities supplied needs to be recorded. Measure the percentage redemption.

Measure the cost of marketing activity versus target. Measure the effect on profit.

Sales promotion

What is it?

It is a short-term event or offer. It is often used for a product launch or relaunch. It may be associated with a cost reduction or a free gift offer. It can apply to a single product or service or a combination of both. It can apply to a whole retail outlet for a one-day sale – such as at Debenhams department store. Fortnum & Mason have a mailshot inviting a list for an evening at their store at a cost of £10 per head, for which respondents are sent a £10 voucher redeemable for purchases on the evening when other offers can be taken up too.

The point-of-sales promotion is to add excitement to an otherwise dull retail environment, offering the customer extra benefits in addition to those that are normally offered. Specialist agencies exist that co-ordinate sales promotions.

In the fashion and clothing industry it is perhaps overplayed with a seeming never-ending rash of sales occurring in a defined shopping area – such as Oxford Street in London.

A sales promotion is sometimes not quite all that it should be with seconds or cheaper goods specially brought in for the sales promotion. It must also be used as a means to clear out-of-date or near-sell-by-date stock.

What can it do?

It can heighten interest and awareness in a particular retail outlet. The sales promotion itself can be used as the focus for additional marketing activity such as PR, advertising or direct marketing such as a mailing or a leaflet handout to increase the benefit. It can be used to attract people who do not usually visit. Harrods and other stores advertise their sales in TV commercials.

The sales promotion can be used to increase traffic past products and services that are not a part of the sales promotion to stimulate their purchase. Sales promotions may be used at the same time by a number of co-located retail outlets.

Measuring achievement

The cost of the sales promotion as a marketing activity some consider should be less than the margin recouped from the extra sales. However it is entirely legitimate to carry out a sales promotion at a loss if that is accepted beforehand – presuming that the loss will be covered by future purchases when people return in a non-sales-promotion time.

Achievement is likely to be measured in terms of extra profit generated as a result of the sales promotion after deduction of the cost of the marketing activities associated with the sales promotion. This is the province of the accountant. The take-up of invitations and redemption of vouchers clearly indicate preferred customers who can be earmarked for future promotions. The seeming VIP status of a special evening itself draws potential customers.

A more useful measure of success may be when the sales promotion is measured against previous sales promotions. The measurement might make comparison of any particular items or range of items that were promoted in the supporting marketing activity to see, over time, which items generated more interest and increased profit and which combination of supporting marketing activities optimised the highest extra profit generated.

Achievement mechanisms

Increased turnover can be measured through normal accounting procedures using the normal turnover as the yardstick. Measure the cost of marketing activity versus target. Measure the effect on profit. Measure the percentage redemption of any vouchers.

Example of a sales promotion disaster – the Hoover free flight offer

In 1993 Hoover offered free flights to UK customers that purchased one of its products. The response was overwhelming and cost the company millions. Its reputation suffered as a consequence.

Packaging

What is it?

Packaging usually consist of several layers applied before a product leaves the place of manufacture. The layers are:

■ Packaging material, used to protect and place the product in position inside the decorative package.
■ A decorative package layer – often printed paper or cardboard, often in a box form that is used to attract potential purchasers; this is the promotional marketing activity about which this section is written.
■ The first outer layer which is usually transparent and for security, both during delivery and for display – it also indicates to the potential purchaser that they have a 'virgin' product straight from the manufacturer. It discourages tampering for whatever purpose.
■ The final layer, or layers, for protection during delivery to the distributor from the supplier.

Packaging of products may have other layers where products are packed in a tray for sale on supermarket shelves often with an additional layer of transparent material to retain the products in the tray. The tray side may also be used as a promotional display.

Packaging can also be applied beneficially to a service. A service, which is an experience, can be packaged in a similar way to a product. An example is the experience of flying in a small aeroplane and perhaps being allowed a short time at the controls 'flying' the aeroplane. The service could just be a turn up, climb in, take off, fly a circuit or two until the time runs out, a landing and return and departure. Packaging the aeroplane experience might include a pre-flight brochure and 'ticket' or voucher with all the details about the aeroplane and the possible flight. During the flight experience, photographs might be taken, which are presented after the flight along with a signed commemoration certificate and a log.

This book is concerned only with the promotional activity associated with the packaging.

It should be noted that there are certain products and services where the packaging should be non-promotional to avoid attention. This applies to products where the recipient does not wish to broadcast their arrival.

A range of larger lingerie – a colourful tampon box

A potential client some years ago, after working for many years in the business, saw an opportunity for the sale of very large sizes of lingerie. The business was established using mail order as the sole means of distribution. The market included many ethnic groups. Had she sought advice or carried out research on the packaging she would have ascertained that discrete parcels were preferred rather than the colourful and descriptive almost brazen packaging she had had designed. Advertising in magazines, not read by her target market, did not help. The sales did not meet forecasts. The business folded.

For a brief period the manufacturer of tampons packaged them in brightly coloured wrappings presumably to make them cheerful and trendy. Women felt embarrassed when taking them out of their handbags or even just when the contents of their handbags was inadvertently disclosed. The brightly coloured packaging was withdrawn.

What can it do?

Like a brochure or an advertisement, packaging can transform a functional product or service into a desirable object. Words and images – particularly photographs – can create an illusion of use in idealized circumstances. Packaging may feature endorsements from other marketing activities – 'as seen on TV'.

Packaging may have to be used to display statutory requirements. Packaging may also have to accommodate instructions for use, if these are not on a separate leaflet with the product or service and may have to be in several languages.

It is a good idea to test packaging as it is to be viewed at typical outlets. If the display shelf is at a distance from the potential customer it will need larger words and images. Small items will often benefit from large packaging; they are less likely to be targets of pilfering but from the marketing viewpoint the more space available means messages can be displayed in a preferred print/design manner.

Packaging is a brand carrier and should conform to the brand values established. It can enhance or maintain the brand values.

Tip on how to start customer relations

People will write for information leaflets and other offers if you advertise/place them on packaging. It may be for related information such as a cookbook, or a how-to-use or for some offer. They will write and happily give you information – see also the market research tip later in this chapter.

You will need to think through how the contact can be developed to offer you future opportunities to sell or obtain information on your customers. Why not offer them the chance to be on your customer panels. This could help with new product development.

Measuring achievement

Packaging should assist the ready sale of the product or service. Measurement of the beneficial effect of packaging is possible, in relation to earlier products or services or to those of competitors both subjectively and through analysis of sales. The effect of the brand will be a major factor.

The real measurement of the benefit of packaging will only be assessed if the product remains the same and the packaging is changed and the change in sales volume is noted.

Achievement mechanisms

The affect of packaging is best assessed using customer panels to endorse and comment on the proposed packaging. Competitor packaging should be similarly assessed. These are market research marketing activities

When new packaging is to be introduced for an existing product, measure the effect over a period of time, including the sales before the new packaging was introduced and afterwards.

Measure cost of marketing activity versus target cost. Measure the effect on profit.

Point of sale (POS)

What is it?

This is the point at which the customer makes the purchase. The environment can include promotional material such as a display video, or demonstrations or sampling to enhance the purchase alongside the product or service. Supermarkets and out-of-town stores offer a range of ways to enhance the product – special displays usually at the ends of shelving between aisles, vertical banners visible the length of an aisle across all shelves – in addition to the tray and product packaging. Leaflets in dispensers (for vouchers, recipes, and so forth) can be added to shelving. Tastings or demonstrations of a product or service are easy to arrange. These can be supported by leaflet handouts near the entrance. All these enhance the point-of-sale promotion.

Ingenious display designs – the work of cardboard engineers – can convert the packaged products container into a stunning eye-catching display. A mix of design and cut-out artistry, print, artwork and colour selection transform the container.

Originally retail outlets were considered as the only points of sale that mattered. Now it is accepted that the point of sale can be at home when a customer buys on the Internet or in future using interactive TV. A self-service machine, even a cashpoint, can be considered a point of sale, which can be enhanced by promotional messages alongside or on screen.

What can it do?

It can attract and persuade the customer to purchase. Particularly useful where a demonstration or sampling is probably a prerequisite to purchase. Useful where the packaging does not allow the benefits or features to be described in readily readable font size. Can help to highlight a new product or new product range or indicate a link to a personality, or film or TV show. In effect it enlarges the visible and other sensory inputs to enhance the impact of the packaging and encourage purchase.

It may be a further idea to use the demonstration or sampling to question the audience immediately afterwards about the product or service.

Measuring achievement

You are probably seeking to prove, through measurement, that the increase in sales and the margin resulting exceeds the cost of the POS marketing activity. The achievement is hopefully more than a flash in the pan with customers in the subsequent months purchasing more of the product or service than previously.

The targets set for increased sales should be based on experience. If experience is lacking then calculate the cost of the break-even sales needed to cover the cost of the marketing activity and use that as a target.

Achievement mechanisms

Sales records need to be kept and analysed over a period from before the POS was initiated and for some time afterwards. Measure the impact on sales on the day and over a period of time.

Measure cost of marketing activity versus target. Measure the effect on profit.

6

One-on-one communication

Sales

What is it?
'Sales' is when people, typically in a retail situation, attempt to assist and persuade a potential customer to make a purchase or to trigger increased sales or to persuade sales of those concept items of higher bottom-line value.

Training of sales staff is the largest benefit to increase turnover and gross profit. In one case an increase in 22 per cent (on the bottom line at a stroke) was achieved through sales staff training (the firm was so delighted that, unfortunately, it did not bother to implement other marketing activities proposed).

Many salespeople have no understanding of either the buying process for the concept – the product or service – for sale or the sales process developed to match. Sales training is often unrelated to the concept. Sales training is better in the franchise or chain catering sector (sandwich, fast food, snacks and branded restaurants), which require training to be carried out in part to meet health and safety standards. As new products and services are introduced then further training should be planned and implemented.

There are standard situations when a salesperson does not make any attempt to sell. Confectionery, tobacconist and newsagents

(CTNs) are examples of this type. The typical corner shop – selling daily commodities. It is the custom and practice to expect no contact with the potential customer. This is probably missing an opportunity as many market-stall traders, car boot sales and village shops know – it is possible to sell more if a dialogue is established.

What can it do?

Where effective sales training is in place, the result is increased turnover and more profitable sales. Effectiveness is when the sales staff fully understand the buyer process and the sales process developed to match, putting across the 'six Cs' to the customer at the appropriate points in time.

Sales training should not just be a one-off activity but should be routinely injected and reinforced.

Measuring achievement

Sales figures from daily or weekly reconciliation will give the gross profit achievement. Comparison of variation of achievement achieved by different persons may give a clue as to the benefit of sales training but be aware of the different hours and days worked.

In the retail sector, the use of 'mystery shoppers' is recognized as an effective way of testing if the concept is properly being sold – particularly for services or a service/product mix. A number of agencies offer a mystery shopper service. Include in the mystery shopper reports any of the range of service items you want checked.

Achievement mechanisms

Measure sales over a period starting from before the sales training was introduced. Use mystery shopper reports over a period of time to compare individual outlets' performance – measure performance and improvements. Compare outlets. In the short term use the successful outlets to understand how the poorer outlets could be improved rather than using the reports to chastise poor performers.

Personal selling

What is it?

Personal selling is when the salesman visits the customer at their premises or at a place other than their own premises. The purpose of the visit is to close a sale and refresh the relationship. Salespeople are equipped with product presenters, order forms and new products to demonstrate. They may occasionally take stock to sell or deliver.

Salespeople usually work to a prearranged schedule of visits based either on area or customer categorization. The schedule will have been confirmed by a series of telephone calls. Occasionally a telephone call may replace a visit but the personal contact and personal benefits that a visit bestows, building on customer relationships such as taking a customer out to lunch, are not foregone lightly. For the salesperson a mix of salary and commission or scale of salary increments based on sales achievement will influence their methods. In addition to salary and commission, salespersons claim expenses relating to travel often based on mileage travelled and subsistence.

Sales are no longer geographically limited. Hong Kong tailors set up shop monthly in the UK hotels, send reminders to existing customers and offer tailored suits, made for a fraction of the UK cost. British salespersons are found in every part of the globe.

There are some salespeople that have been known to extend the monies claimed beyond the true expenses incurred. The reasons for such behaviour are often complex. It is important to bear in mind that the rules set are often considered fair game – to optimize claims by salespeople. A salesperson who decides to leave a firm or is given notice may seek to optimize the salary/commission and expenses mix for their final period of employment by obtaining sales that less discerning clients accept and are then unable to sell on to their own customers or to use themselves. Subsequent recriminations, if not handled well, can lead to an end to a customer relationship and even to the customer ceasing to be a customer.

Some salespeople have set up business on their own and act as agents for a number of firms. This may seem sense as it saves on many salespeople visiting the same customers; the weakness is that the inclination will be to sell more of the products from the firm that remunerates at a higher rate or whose products are easiest to sell – agents tend to optimize their effort to obtain the highest return overall. Occasionally salespeople employed by competing firms will combine and visit mutual customers on behalf of all to save their own time – for example cigarette and tobacco product salespeople from competing organizations have been known to meet at a motorway service station and then one visits confectionery, tobacconist and newspaper (CTN) outlets on behalf of all of them. This collusion depends on the individual salesperson's beliefs; arrangements such as this only flourish with poor supervision.

What it can do?
Customer relationships can be developed and 'bonding' develops between the salesperson and the buyer. This bonding is difficult to break and order taking is assured, particularly for new products introduced.

Training salespeople is important in the buying and sales process introduced to match. The salesperson must also be trained to recognize the opportunities for selling other products and services and for the take-up of referrals.

Using salespeople, as one marketing activity among many, should be part of an integrated marketing plan. They should be aware of other marketing activities and their sales call plans should be adjusted to take account of advertising, public relations and direct mail or any marketing activities. They can be used to recommend the instigation of any direct marketing activity and to follow it up.

The importance of sales training – examples of success and shortfall for sales calls

A salesperson selling software was accompanied by another on a sales call. The salesperson arrived at the customer's premises and rapidly arranged the four customer representatives in a semicircle. After a very short personal introduction the customer representatives were asked to introduce themselves and to explain the system need as they saw it and the present shortfalls they had observed. Each salesperson then demonstrated the software product carefully ensuring every shortfall described was covered and then went round the semicircle confirming that the shortfalls raised had been covered, at the same time repeating the benefits and the features of the software. An order was always secured using this sales process – effectively establishing the buyer's needs and matching the sales process to it (as described earlier). The salesperson had developed a kneepad-affixed presenter to ease the process and allow hands-free operation while maintaining the attention of prospective customers.

Another firm selling a service was unsure of the claims of competence of one of their salespeople and a sales call was accompanied. The salesperson did not allow sufficient journey time and so arrived late. Instead of taking in the pointers within the reception area to the potential customer's abilities and provenance (they had received awards, had a French parent company and an all-female staff) the salesperson plunged directly into how every firm was pretty awful and only the service that he was trying to sell would make them reasonable or better. The salesperson then used male examples related to the service provided by the potential customer and by chance told an unfortunate story about Paris and its business and leisure activities. As the salesperson was being ushered out, he remembered the excellent presenter supplied by the client for the first time and for a few moments obtained some redemption. But no order was placed for the service. The salesperson had the grace to confess that no preparation had been made for the sales call – but, despite further training, he did not improve and left the company not long after.

The use of salespersons visiting firms may be limited in future in some sales categories. The advent of the Internet has meant that it is possible to show considerable product ranges and product details, even demonstrating them with video clips, to would-be buyers on a Web site. The Web buyer can add them to a virtual 'shopping basket' and place an order. Web sites now allow payment. The computer industry is not surprisingly fairly converted to Internet selling – supplementing the Web site sales with catalogue and call centre order taking. In addition, some firms produce their catalogues on CD ROM – with built-in Web ordering.

Although the demise of the salesperson is forecast in some categories, the known benefit of a salesperson's capability to establish lasting customer relationships leading to bonding with customers should not be forgotten.

Measuring achievement

The cost of employing a salesperson should be considerably less than the business that person brings in and the profit that they generate. The hidden costs of employing salespeople should be included, such as supervision, processing claims, the cost of administration – converting an order into a completed sale (the Internet by comparison costs next to nothing).

In an integrated marketing campaign, including salespeople carrying out sales calls, it may be easiest to ring-fence the campaign so their part in securing orders can be measured and their improved contribution set against previous periods, while the cost of all the contributing marketing activities is added to the cost of employing them themselves.

Salespeople need to be closely controlled. The damage that poor sales calls can generate cannot be underestimated and sales-call performance should be monitored with the customer (see the rubber glove theory examples earlier). Any personality clashes should be monitored and remedied by transferring customer responsibility to another salesperson. Salespeople's remuneration should be carefully calculated to be mutually beneficial to them and to the firm. Where they are not able to perform to match their set targets, then, if any remedial training is unsuccessful, they should be released from their contract. When recruiting salespersons, great care should be taken, particularly taking up references and ensuring they are genuine and positive.

Agent remuneration should be drawn up in a contract that is mutually beneficial, with targets set for performance in the long term and for an initial trial period, based on order taking, which match the period of the year and the distribution potential. Setting a trial period is always helpful.

Achievement mechanisms

Measure the sales orders taken by day and time, by customer, by area. Measure trends. Compare with previous periods and previous years. Compare salespersons by area by category and in comparisons with other salespersons. Compare sales achievements with and without any other marketing activities within integrated marketing campaigns.

Salespeople as any other staff will have annual work objectives set and these should be appraised as normal. Measure the cost of marketing activity versus target. Measure the effect on profit.

An example of salespeople using opportunities arising from lax management scrutiny

A firm employing 1,100 salespeople decided arbitrarily to halve the mileage allowance paid as an expense. The salespeople as a body decided to double the mileage figures on all claims they made by way of retaliation. This state of affairs continued for some time. The firm then introduced computerization and all claims were computer processed. Then salespersons were told to take their company cars in for tyre changing as the computer assessed that from the mileage indicated the tyres were worn. The salespersons felt they could not confess to their fraudulent claim making and compounded their troubles by arranging for an intermediary to purchase the part-worn tyres and to sell them at a profit from which they further benefited. The next step came when their cars were ordered in for exchange. A further intermediary bought and resold the cars at their correct mileage. Only when the routine employment of a sales investigator occurred did the fact that the mileage on the company cars did not reflect the distances claimed come to light: 1,100 salespeople lost their jobs.

Exhibitions, trade fairs

What are they?
An exhibition is usually held separately for the trade and for customers. Selling is not allowed at exhibitions. Sometimes there are trade-only days within a mixed exhibition. The difference is important in that the contact time is considerably different between the two types; typically of the order of one or two minutes contact time only for a customers – usually consumers – as against the trade, where typical contact time may be around 20 minutes. When Autotech, the trade exhibition for the motor industry, was

first organized, manufacturers and suppliers assumed that the motor show parameters applied – stands manned by attractive scantily clad women dishing out glossy brochures. Now Autotech is manned by women who are chartered-engineers with a full understanding of the highly technical products and capable of discussing matters for hours if needed.

Exhibitions are generally held by trade and by category. Sometimes a number of categories are combined and held simultaneously, such as for the Spring and Autumn Fairs held at the National Exhibition Centre. An example of a single category exhibition is the UK Toy Fair, held at the end of January at the Excel site in Docklands. The UK Toy Fair is one of four international toy fairs closely linked by succeeding dates when toys for the following year, but principally for Christmas, are displayed and orders taken.

Sometimes most order taking for some categories is carried out at an exhibition – the early February Spring Fair is when most purchasing of calendars for the following year takes place. A new company selling calendars to the retail trade in the UK may only be able to find buyers prepared to order calendars at that exhibition almost to the exclusion of the rest of the year – with any ongoing sales sold to the same designs through merchandisers. The corollary is that to sell calendars widely in the UK will require attendance with a stand at the trade fair.

For every category there is one or more exhibitions held. To find out what exhibitions are held and where, there are specialist exhibition trade guides. The trade magazines and exhibition venues also list exhibitions held.

Exhibition stands are allowed on station concourses and shopping malls. These are usually arranged on a one-to-one basis between the station or mall operator and the exhibitor.

Not to be confused with exhibitions are shows, fairs (not just for trade), markets and car boot sales/garage sales. Some well-known exhibition venues are used for shows and fairs which may add to the confusion. There are also opportunities to sell to consumers at more recent shows sponsored by the media – including TV – mimicking the Ideal Home Show, sponsored by a newspaper. The BBC sponsors DIY, homemaking and fashion shows. There are a number of county shows and ones with a central attraction such as steam or agriculture or 'country themed' fairs. Markets are regular and often permanently established places where stalls/stands are available for hire controlled by councils or licensed operators. (For example, Covent Garden where a stall can be hired on a one-day-per-week basis.) Car boot sales allow members of the public sometimes to set up their own stands alongside trade stalls at regular sites. Garage sales are individual enterprises.

What can they do?

An exhibition can allow customers to handle, view, experience, sample, test, try, ask questions about and place orders for products and services. Careful selection of the exhibition (by category and trade) should ensure that plenty of the target market for your concept – products and services – will be attending. This does not mean that they will visit your stand or place orders – even if they have done so previously.

The design of the stand requires an understanding of the objectives set for attendance at the exhibition. It is important to consider the size and location within the exhibition area and the stand manning to cope with expected numbers. It is better to start small and learn from experience when considering stand size. If a part of the purpose is to understand customers' problems in detail and discuss possible product or service solutions then it may be important to include an area where there are limited distractions and a degree of perceived confidentiality is possible (Helmsmen suggest a particular design of booth that both hides and 'traps' the prospect, minimizes distractions and is relatively soundproof, yet allows an eye to be kept on the remainder of the stand by the stand person talking to the prospect; the booth has a small footprint). It is a good idea, if many brief discussions are likely to be required with prospective customers, to seat those manning that part of the stand on seats that place them at eye level with customers. This avoids fatigue. People are unhappy talking up or down to each other, preferring near-horizontal eye contact. Areas of stand visible down aisles should have lettering large enough to be read at a distance with short crisp messages putting across concept benefits as 'attention getters'.

As a generalization based on observation both from attendance and stand manning over many years most people on exhibition stands have received little or inappropriate training to 'sell' at exhibitions. Training can enhance the sales performance several times (Helmsmen's clients have increased order taking by a factor of three or four after training – the selling process at exhibitions is covered in outline in an earlier section in this book). Training should be designed to impart an understanding of the different types of customer visiting the stand and the sales process to match those types – again described earlier in this book.

An exhibition should be part of an integrated marketing activities campaign with advertising, PR and direct contact marketing activities planned alongside both sequentially and concurrently.

Example of an ill-considered purpose of an exhibition stand – financial services

A company in the financial services sector prior to becoming a client had arranged a stand at a Money Show at Earls Court. The purpose was to obtain more high-value customers.

The result had been the acquisition of the names and addresses of more consumers than they could tackle over several years. Few of them were high value. The small amount of business obtained did not cover the cost of the stand.

The selection of the Money Show was unfortunate in terms of the target audience attending – they did not match the customer profile of customers sought by the company. The volume of consumers attending far exceeded the handling capability.

Alternative marketing activities produced more high-value clients in numbers the company could handle.

Measuring achievement
Clearly the purpose of the exhibition stand will to an extent determine what should be measured. The aim may be to acquire a target number of orders for your products and services. The order-taking success may include those taken at the exhibition itself or include orders that can be attributed to the customer attending the exhibition but ordering subsequently. The purpose may be to elicit a target number of enquiries or to create a database of potential customers from exhibition visitors.

The successful achievement of the exhibition may be to make either a gross or a net profit from the exhibition – a positive figure arising for either orders less costs, or profit on orders less costs.

Participation in the exhibition may be a part of a brand value awareness exercise. In which case a target of awareness improvement could be set.

Achievement mechanisms

Exhibition attendance figures can be obtained from the organizers. Stand footfall can be measured with a visitor counter or using a box for business cards (with a raffle prize?) or stapling cards to enquiry forms or writing down names and details of stand visitors and subsequently counting them. Order numbers and order values by customer resulting both at the exhibition and from subsequent marketing activity – as long as that activity is encompassed within the ring fence of the exhibition – should be reasonably readily obtained. Long-term customers resulting from initial contact at exhibitions can be measured as long as a field in the database indicates that the customer was acquired at the exhibition.

To acquire a true picture of cost it is necessary to ring-fence the marketing activities carefully. Training and staff costs for the exhibition should be added in along with the supporting marketing activities such as direct mailing, advertising, PR, stand literature costs and the costs of the space, the stand and the equipment.

To measure an improvement in awareness resulting from the exhibition campaign activity a survey of your target market will need to be conducted before and after the exhibition.

Measure the cost of marketing activity versus target. Measure the effect on profit.

Conferences, lectures and seminars

What are they?

Conferences and seminars are occasions when potential customers are invited to listen to speakers on subjects of interest to them, usually within their category or trade sector. The speakers may be from outside organizations – particularly for a conference. A seminar may include just speakers from inside your firm.

Typically a conference or seminar is held in a purpose-built centre or local hotel with refreshments and opportunities to network. It is entirely possible to run a conference or seminar as a marketing activity. A part of the conference can be used as a product or service launch. The remainder containing subject matrial perhaps leading up to defining a need that the new product or service satisfies.

Larger conferences may be organized by trade bodies or business associations or by professional conference organizations. Sometimes such a conference is associated with an exhibition. Exhibition stands offering concepts associated with the conference subject are set out in areas adjoining the conference hall.

The opportunity to speak at a conference organized by others may arise. This should be treated as a PR activity. It is generally unwise to use it as a sales pitch opportunity.

There is a Kogan Page book on *How to Run a Successful Conference* by John Fisher.

What can they do?
It can establish intellectual and academic credibility alongside professional competence.

A professional services client of Helmsmen has now held several series of lectures; each series including the leading authoritative person to speak on the areas of competence that exist within the client firm. Each invited delegate is hosted and entertained and given the opportunity to meet the speakers. The senior partner has now been invited to speak on many occasions. The client surveys measure ever-increasing status and an improved ranking among similar professional firms by both customers and intermediaries.

The subject content of the conference, lecture or seminar should be based on experience, knowledge, or feature research into the subject.

The purpose of holding a conference, lecture or seminar is usually not overt sales but where the product or service is raised it is generally accepted as reasonable to describe objectively the benefits and features of it to potential customers. Often the purpose is to improve awareness and establish and foster relationships with customers or potential customers.

Measuring achievement
The measurement has usually to be in the form of market research in varying degrees to ascertain whether the purpose is achieved.

Repeat attendance over time is an indication of success of a conference, seminar or lecture series.

Achievement mechanisms

A straightforward measurement is to measure response to invitations. Measure how many attended, measure how many responded positively, measure how many were invited. Maintain records of those attending, both existing and potential customers and the subject matter and attendance over a period of time. Record conversions to customer. It may be possible to ask attendees to complete a questionnaire at the end. Record and analyse responses to the questionnaires.

A telephone call can be made shortly afterwards, primarily about an alternative subject, but the subject is switched to include reference to the conference, lecture or seminar and ascertain feedback as to value. (This switching topics is a technique favoured by journalists, particularly radio journalists such as those on the *Today* programme on Radio 4.)

Client surveys can ascertain customer perception and views as to their rating of the firm and its professional service and competence in academic and intellectual terms.

Measure the cost of marketing activity versus target.

Incentives

What are they?

Incentives in the context of this book are used to enhance staff performance and motivate their marketing activities, particularly personal selling. Incentives reward performance that is above the minimum expected.

The subject is included here for completeness. Incentives for customers are described in this book as promotions.

One company, for example, operates a travel incentive business that typically offers a range of improving travel options as incentives as salespersons achieve sales targets.

A Kogan Page book by John Fisher, *How to Run Successful Incentive Schemes*, covers travel incentive vouchers, merchandise bonus, shares and smart cards designed to increase your staff motivation and performance.

What can they do?
They improve your staff performance, particularly in highly
competitive commodity product categories and hence such
improvement should follow through to profit.

Measuring the achievement
You are looking for an improvement in turnover and hence
improved profit after deduction of the incentive marketing activity
cost.

Achievement mechanisms
Measure the percentage improvement on sales before and after the
introduction of the incentive scheme. Measure the cost of marketing activity versus target. Measure the effect on profit.

Product launch (the same also applies to service launch)

What is it?
A special occasion when a new concept is first made public or
displayed to a selected media and customer audience. The impact
is heightened by adding personalities or some stunt to attract
attention.

It is usually a marketing activity associated with PR. It is most
effective when the product or service is technically, or in its service
parameters, quite different from any existing concept – that is
product or service. It is less effective when a me-too concept, that is
one that is similar to existing concepts, is launched. It is also effective when an existing brand is extended to cover another category
or product class.

What can it do?
A product launch can capture media coverage that is particularly
connected with your target market. This media coverage provides
objective comment that has more credibility than using advertisements. You do not need all the media, it may be sufficient to your
needs to capture the attention of the trade press that covers your
concept. For consumer products the consumer press will need to
be attracted to attend the launch.

The launch activity must be considered in detail with every
contingency explored and the launch activity rehearsed. Journalist

transport arrangements must allow for the exigencies of the weather.

A product launch can produce a higher awareness of a concept than spending on any other marketing activity and in a shorter time. It is also short-lived and the impact will rapidly fade away.

To sustain and build on the awareness other marketing activities should follow. Advertising and persuading editors to commission articles might be considered.

Example of a product launch – the Dyson washing machine

The Dyson launch of the new washing machine was saved by the lifting of the cloudbase sufficient to fly the helicopters carrying journalists in to Malmesbury from London. History does not yet record whether any alternative transport arrangements would have succeeded if the cloudbase had not lifted.

After the Dyson launch – a report in *Which?* magazine proved ideal for Dyson, maintaining the impact of the new washing machine in the public domain for some time at no further cost.

Measuring achievement

For product launches, immediately observable effects on brand measures like awareness and sales are usual.

A product launch can be supported by advertising. Evidence suggests that the stronger the advertising in support of the product launch, the greater the benefit to sales. When using advertising in support of a product launch to ascertain the effect of the advertising alone you may need to measure the total change in sales then deduct the effect of other measurable marketing activities to find out the advertising contribution.

For example, for marketing activities such as PR in support of the product launch measure the amount, extent and breadth of editorial comment that results comparing it with the equivalent cost of advertising in those media. Mention of the product launch as a news item is a considerable achievement rather than just appearing in articles. That is why high-profile product launches are considered valuable – they have the potential to breach media areas and coverage not normally accessible. See also the PR marketing activity later in this chapter.

In effect the essence of the success of a product launch is probably best measured by the likely sales take-up without a product launch as against the sales achieved with a product launch.

A way to measure the impact of a product launch might be to inform and demonstrate a new concept to a number of customers in confidence and then ask them to place orders. Subsequently see if their orders are increased as a result of the product launch.

Market research through questionnaires can confirm the extent of awareness of the features and benefits of the new concept.

Achievement mechanisms

Market research after a product launch will give an idea of its short-term achievement. If the market research is a regular feature then the effect on the brand can also be measured. Measure the cost of marketing activity versus target.

Call centre

What is it?

A firm offering a telephone answering service responding to telephone enquiries. A call centre is the inbound service – the opposite of telemarketing, which is outbound. (See telemarketing, earlier.) Call centre operators operate with a tree-form pre-agreed script obtaining information from the caller during the call as well as responding with appropriate information.

For one company, the call centre staff obtained information regarding where the caller had seen the telephone number, the caller's name, address and postcode, the time and date of call, and gave out information giving the name and telephone number of their nearest supplier and an alternative. The call centre staff had been briefed about the client product and were able to answer general queries as required. The telephone number appeared in editorials, advertisements, inserts, mailshots and on the Web site. The supplier subsequently redeemed a voucher offer.

The call centre staff can be trained to appear to be a part of your firm. They are able to increase the number of persons answering calls should a surge arise and perhaps divert calls to other call centres if the demand goes beyond that. Call centres should be notified of marketing activities dates when the target audience is to be 'hit'.

Call centre staff log all calls and provide both the log and an analysis of the data collected in a variety of formats for each period (typically a week) and comparing each week with every previous week.

What can it do?

It is a cost-effective way of providing a professionally trained response to customer callers. Customers can be either business or consumers, existing or potential customers. The call centre brief should be clear about the objectives. The database of interested potential customers is useful in any case both to you and to suppliers.

Careful consideration of the order and content of call centre responses allowing flexibility of response makes customers perceive that they are leading the conversation while actually having information extracted from them to meet the objectives.

The telephone line may be either a free phone or local call line rather than a national call charge line to encourage prospective callers to make the call. The call centre will have a number of lines available, which can be used – it is important to get the number right in all marketing material.

The call centre can often be used to confirm that other marketing activities have happened as agreed.

Measuring achievement

Usually a response target is set. The call centre managers have experience and can give advice about the likely response. This may be no more than a return of the order of a direct mailshot. Promotions and voucher redemption may increase the response numbers.

Where the service involves contact with your customers such as calls between customers and call centre staff, then it is important that the script they are using matches your brand values. It is important to train them in your company ethos – take a range of products to the call centre team and demonstrate them. This happens rarely, but product demonstrations are really beneficial to give an understanding of your products that can be used when the call centre staff talk to your potential customers. It is a motivator to the call centre staff to see the products they are taking calls about.

The call centre can be used as an intermediate measurement for a number of activities. For example, the measurement of the number of customers actually redeeming vouchers at suppliers was the target for one marketing activity – there was a correlation between take-up and supplier distance from customer. This correlation exercise was achieved using call centre data. A review of distribution resulted and additional suppliers were found to improve national coverage.

Measuring the differing response levels to different marketing activities all linked through a call centre can be a helpful and cost-effective way of assessing achievement. Call centre staff can assist with suggestions .

Achievement mechanisms

Call centre logs should provide data as agreed. Analysis of the data will allow measurements such as regional interest, perceptions of price and value, and comprehension or otherwise of the product or service offered.

Call centres measure other marketing activities. Call records analysis can confirm that an advertising regional insert has indeed gone to a region. Measure the cost of marketing activity versus target.

A cautionary tale

A two-page advertorial for a company was supported by an insert in a magazine. For technical reasons the magazine could only include the insert over two issues – the North of England and Scotland areas were to receive the insert one month later than the rest of the UK.

The publisher stated later that all had gone to plan and over the two months further certification was received from the printer that the inserts had all been placed as agreed. However, all the calls received by the call centre responding to the second insert came from South West postcodes. After four months of denial the publisher admitted that the certification was incorrect and the insert placement had gone wrong through a management error and indeed owned up to a further error; 25,000 fewer copies than planned had been distributed. The client obtained a further advertorial and a refund by way of compensation.

A call centre can confirm claims made by publishers and printers concerning insertions and advertisement coverage.

7

General communications

Newsprint/magazine advertising, inserts

What is it?

It is the purchase of print space in a newspaper or magazine that displays information about your product or service. It can also be your own printed material inserted using the magazine as a carrier. The insert produced usually has to conform to a specification set by the publisher. There are two basic types of space sold – display and classified. Classified is primarily for members of the public or small businesses to advertise and the advertisement is dictated or faxed to fit a template within a matrix of other classified ads.

Each publisher, usually through the display advertising manager, will send a rate card and data concerning the specification of the printed material and often samples – back numbers of the magazine – and marketing information about the readership and how the magazine beats competitor titles. Advertisement placing within a magazine or newspaper decides its cost. Inserts are similarly rated. A number of newspapers – the weekend titles in particular – now wrap the colour supplements and inserts in a bag. This avoids inserts falling out.

Advertorials are advertisements written, designed and produced by the newspaper's own staff. This often makes them look as if they are part of the written contents – and the presumption is that they are more likely to be read.

Test an insert – say 50,000 out of 500,000. Use 'tip-ons' in preference to a cut-out voucher (see Chapter 5).

Other forms of advertising included in this chapter (see below) but not under this heading are posters, transport advertising, radio and TV advertising

What can it do?

Before deciding to advertise it is important to determine that the magazine or newspaper readership matches your target customers and that the customers do read it – ask a sample where possible. There are some 9,000 titles of magazines in the UK alone so it is important to get it right. In London there are 220 or so newspapers of which about half are distributed free; UK-wide there are many more newspaper titles than actual productions, with the same basic editorial content being published in different local titles – your display advertisement could appear in consequence in several papers in a group of newspapers owned by one publisher.

There are many research studies (principally carried out in Germany) where observations have been made as to how people read magazines and newspapers. These seem to conclude that Western-educated persons read articles in a newspaper in an arc following the letter C reversed starting from the top. Whether people read or even take in an advertisement is a moot point. A quick test is to take back a magazine and ask people to name any one advertisement in the magazine. The use by Bennetton of shocking photographs may be one way to be noticed – outrage or humour may work far better than a straightforward message.

Measuring achievement

Why you are advertising should determine what you are going to measure. The magazine will provide circulation and readership figures and a profile of its readers – these should match your customer profile – measure it!

Advertising sells by giving customers news – that is, by creating a desire by reminding them about the concept; or by building further customer expectations and values. So, justifying the advertising budget needs to be related to the defined advertising marketing activity.

For advertisements seeking to increase or maintain sales the measure of success should be just that. You will need to have measurement mechanisms to measure existing sales levels and any surge or increase as a result of the advertisements. For the dot.com company in the earlier example the surge of visits to the Web site was large but short lived as a result of the advertisements – sadly, neither the advertisement nor the Web site persuaded many people to buy, insufficient to remain in business. The failure may have been due to not matching the buying process or the fact that the 'six Cs' did not add up for potential buyers.

Advertisements that just include a message to change attitude or increase awareness but without a response mechanism can be measured by market research. The research needs to be carried out before and after the advertisement appears.

Advertisements that include a response mechanism should be set targets of response.

There are specialist companies that measure advertising value for money; see www.mediaudits.com.

Achievement mechanisms
Measure the (increased!) sales by area, by category, by measuring the sales prior to an advertisement appearing and afterwards.

If the advertising seeks to change attitudes or increase awareness then qualitative market research should be applied before and afterwards. Measure the increase.

If the advertisement directs people to a Web site, track and measure hits. Increases should respond to advertisement appearances. The duration may reflect the use of newspaper (very short) against magazine (longer) falling back when the next issue comes out. Measure the cost of marketing activity versus target. Measure the effect on profit.

Public relations (PR)

What is it?
This is the marketing activity that tries to develop understanding between an organization and its public. It is often associated purely with the media – reaching journalists and editors through press releases – but in fact it covers any marketing activity that tries to put across the views of your organization, even employees,

shareholders, analysts, but as a marketing activity it generally excludes any form of advertising and direct communication with individuals. It may be run in-house or through an agency or a mix of both. An agency will often be a specialist dealing with a particular tranche of the media, for example sport, or food and drink. See below for comment on agencies.

Public relations has been overlooked by many not only in the marketing function but as an essential tool in creating increased revenue for a business. This has been partly due to the poor quality and lack of training of many of the disciplines' practitioners, but also because of the lack of measurement. While PR had the support of someone of influence on the board, there was little need to assess its contribution to the bottom line. Indeed, for many years, a heavy, well-presented, press cuttings book was usually enough to get the budget increased for the following year.

In today's more tightly controlled business environment this is not nearly enough, although it is a sad fact, and astonishing to this author, that so many practitioners are still trying to justify their efforts and results by equating media coverage with the corresponding advertising space ratio. This has always been a shortcoming as it not only reduces the awareness of public relations to the same level as purchased advertising space. The idea that a two-column, positive story about a company in the *Financial Times* is only as important as the same space taken up by an advertisement, is naive in the extreme.

Readers have become adept at differentiating between a genuine third party assessment (which amounts to an independent endorsement) in editorial form and an agency-designed, paid-for piece of publicity (or propaganda). In addition, the basic cost of PR is vastly different from even an adequate advertising budget. Comparatively speaking a couple of articles or photos, or even mention in a feature, may well have considerable impact plus the authenticity and authority of the above-mentioned, independent endorsement.

It has been proved that consistent mentions in editorials have a cumulative effect on the perceptions of a marketplace that intermittent advertising has difficult in achieving. Despite the amount of computer software available for design and easy access to media contacts, for the message to be credible needs specialist skills in writing, layout and promotion. The approach should always be to define achievable objectives and a viable timescale before even attempting to define the level of expenditure.

A PR marketing activity can be a high-profile event or a continuous drip feed of stories to build a relationship with your particular media – a mix of local area and specialist media related to your business interests. The importance of drip-feed PR is often overlooked, both inside and outside PR. High-profile events are the glamour end of PR. The ongoing PR builds up a reputation in times when all is going well that stands you in good stead when a crisis occurs. In times of famine the hard work pays dividends.

Generally a press release has to meet the 'oh really' criteria applied by a journalist or editor to be accepted for publication. 'Oh really' means that the story is timely, appropriate, relevant to the readers and different. If the story does not merit an 'oh really' do not be surprised if it is 'spiked'. It must also conform to a particular format and should be just factual. It is wiser to use someone who has experience of getting stories into papers than to attempt to do it oneself. There are a number of good books on the subject – see Appendix 1.

The advantage of an accepted press release is that it is free. Be aware that some publishers have recently been trying to extract cash for photographs to accompany an editorial. This should be resisted.

What can it do?
Public relations can lead to coverage of a happening at no direct cost other than the cost of the marketing activity.

Press relations is what PR firms are actually best at and what they should be used for. Some PR people may have a view that they are all that is required and that marketing and advertising are superfluous but that is unwise as firms still have to have headed paper and send out letters and train sales staff and receptionists, which are not PR activities.

PR can get messages put across in print that would not pass the Advertising Standards Authority's requirements as an advertisement. Public relations can use innuendo successfully.

The cost of the PR marketing activity has achieved a return of some five to six times the outlay if the same space had been bought as advertising. In practice the effect on the brand and the impact is probably greater than the pure financial assessment. Editorial copy has greater impact in credibility terms than an advertisement – advertorials may be purchased from the advertising side of magazines (see above).

To measure the achievement

The placing of the ring fence is important to measure the achievement of PR-associated marketing activities. In truth it may be best to consider ring-fencing a campaign – that is a bundle of marketing activities which include PR. The ring fence should be separate for routine PR and for high-profile PR-related events such as a product launch.

A PR marketing activity should cover staff cost and expense. If you are using a PR agency the cost will be apparent – though you may need to add the cost of whoever is your in-house point of contact.

Financial return may be measured by simply estimating the cost of the coverage in terms of an equivalent display advertisement of the same size and in the same place in the paper or magazine. This is not the full benefit. The messages that appear are often ones that you could not achieve through advertising. You may wish to weight the coverage more favourably for editorial than the advertising rate. Experience over time will indicate what the weighting factor should be.

Routine market research of customers should rate the value of your brand more highly with time as the editorial coverage impacts. The same value rating will not be achieved through advertising. Should an adverse editorial or article appear then the effect should similarly be measured – the impact on your brand and the impact on sales.

A number of important techniques have been developed to assess and measure the ability of PR to actually change consumer beliefs and actions. Refined use of these techniques and feedback research can also prove a change in revenue impact on the bottom line. Investment in brand and revenue building PR activities can be measured by assessing the customers' willingness to purchase from your firm and not the competition. Customers' attitudes about a company or product is strongly linked to their purchasing decisions and care has to be taken to make sure the level of investment in marketing takes great account of the credibility of the media being used for the message.

A number of British companies have taken the measurement of PR effectiveness by developing 'measurement kits' to not only track consumer or stakeholder attitudes but also media targeting and impact. The various techniques measure not only how many people receive a message, but the quality of it, its prominence and the direction and size of its exposure. This means that the PR effect can be isolated from other marketing activities.

It is worth using a cutting where a mention has been made of your firm – particularly if you are sending out press releases on a wide distribution. The PR agency will suggest it in any case. The cuttings service records every occasion when your name appears. Some cuttings services send a copy of each cutting including placing – that is, where it appeared in the media.

Achievement mechanisms

Measure the coverage by range of magazines, journals and newspapers and relate to each press release sent out. Measure the equivalent cost of placing advertisements in those publications (using rate and data cards). Measure through market research the impact on the brand – attitude and perspective. Measure the effect on profit and the cost of marketing activity versus target.

Market research

What is it?

It is the collection of information about customers and potential customers to assist decision taking or confirm decision taking. *The Economist Pocket Marketing* book gives the following reasons for market research:

- measurement of marketing potential;
- determination of market characteristics;
- market share analysis;
- sales analysis;
- studies of business trends;
- competitive product studies;
- short-range (up to one year) and long-range forecasting;
- new product potential and acceptance;
- pricing studies;
- testing of existing products;
- establishing sales quotas and territories.

It is often carried out through the use of a questionnaire. The questionnaire is completed by personal interview, by post, through the Internet or by telephone. (A free trial CD ROM provided by Mercator Systems is included with this book to aid the construction of a questionnaire. An Internet questionnaire version is also available.)

Market research may be carried out using in-house staff (who should be appropriately trained) or through the use of an agency – see above – which can be briefed and used to carry out market research. There is a body – the Market Research Society – whose members abide by and operate a code of practice.

There are two basic types of research – qualitative and quantitative. Qualitative research takes in interviews, hall tests, discussion groups to discover the attitude, perception and motivation of customers – it does not produce significant statistical results. Qualitative research is useful to elicit desirable and undesirable features of new products. Quantitative research uses sampling techniques to find what proportion of the target population do what, such as how many households have a PC. There are about eight base parameters for quantitative research – who are you, what and where do you buy, how much and at what price, when, what else might you have bought and where?

There are omnibus surveys to which an organization's market research questions can be added for a proportional share of the cost. Tracking surveys follow a brand over a prolonged period.

What can it do?
You need to be clear what is the problem on which you need market research help to make your decision:

■ Market research can measure attitude changes. To find out the effect of the change you need to measure before you carry out the marketing activity and afterwards (as Mark Dixon, MD of Regus, did in the example given earlier).
■ Market research can assess customer preference for new products.
■ Market research can identify the way that customers see concepts and give an indication of the language that they use to describe the concept. The perception is likely to be different from your expectations (see self recognition criteria described

earlier). The feedback from this research is useful to feed back as marketing messages.

■ Market research can determine the preference for communication media channels of your potential customers. It can save wasted resource in advertising in the wrong magazine or at the wrong time.

■ Market research can measure brand bonding – how many of your customers never buy from anyone else? Research shows that of the high-value customers of one supermarket, 43 per cent never shop anywhere else. This is a high brand-bonding level. Clearly the supermarket can identify high-average-value customers on the basis of the amount they spend and their frequency of purchasing. Market research has then to ask the question: do they ever shop anywhere else? Then find out how many other high-value customers do the same until you have a sample sufficient to be statistically valid. Brand bonding consists of five elements all of which market research can measure. Shortfalls in any one of the five can indicate the marketing objectives that need to be addressed and the marketing activities to improve the bonding. This is a task for the marketing consultant.

■ Market research is not necessarily expensive. A client survey for a professional firm calling around 12 clients by telephone to obtain views about the service, brand and provide answers to other questions may take around two days of time including preparing a short report. This small sample can indicate whether there is the need for further research. If the response is consistent then the results will give very useful output. If it is inconsistent then a much wider sample will be required but it also means that the experience of your concept varies considerably, which should be worrying.

Do not be surprised at how much information people will give you. They volunteer information as well so leave space for additional comments.

Market research tip

A valuable tip: enclose a small folded questionnaire leaflet with every product or service and await responses. It is quite amazing how many people will take the time to fill it in and send it to you, paying the postage themselves. Businesses report they receive up to 200 returned completed questionnaires per month per product. This is an amazingly useful and inexpensive piece of market research. You can ask where the product was purchased, how they heard about it, how long they have used it. The results should be analysed and trends plotted.

Do not forget that from the day you started trading you are building up data in-house that can be used to supply market research needs with information. Remember the adventurous travel company example where in-house records over 10 years clearly showed that more than 50 per cent of business was from repeats and referrals. All that was then needed was a way to exploit that fact.

Measuring achievement

Success is when the market research findings give you the information on which you are able to make your decision.

Perhaps the cost of not arriving at the right decision, the saving in terms of business failure, is a measurement of achievement in terms of the value of the market research marketing activity. For example, if the decision is to decide to promote either concept A or concept B, what is the cost of proceeding with each? Whatever sum is spent on market research will probably save a multiple of that if the wrong decision is made.

Market research will be needed to measure whether a marketing activity has had any effect on awareness or attitude or perception. The research will need to be carried out twice: before and after the marketing activity. If you do not find out whether a marketing activity has given any value then it will be a waste of the money spent on it and any future money you spend on similar marketing activities.

Achievement mechanisms

Measure the cost of the marketing research versus the cost of making a wrong decision. Measure the cost of not knowing whether a marketing activity has given you value or not. Measure the cost of the marketing activity against the target.

Agencies

What are they?

An agency is the body of expertise that will take your brief on advertising, PR, market research or whatever and convert it into a package of marketing activities that will effectively communicate with appropriate audiences to gain good value for money. Some agencies have combined and offer all activities including direct marketing and the new media.

The recognition that integrated marketing is the future on the marketing communications side has led a number of agencies to scrap the old distinction of being above or below the line only, and starting at the top (Saatchi & Saatchi) a transformation is occurring whereby all marketing communication alternatives are offered within one umbrella body (a collection of differing specialism agencies) or firm. With PR firms there is much specialism and it is important to be very sure that the PR firm does cover the category areas and industry sectors you are interested in.

Gone are the days when the offer of a parking place in central London secured the agency the deal. The agency is now keener to be seen to provide value for money. With little prompting they should also offer to measure their achievement.

There is a book *Getting the Best from Agencies and Other Outside Services*, by Geoffrey Smith (1994), published by Kogan Page, with further detailed information on the subject. The arguments for using in-house staff versus an agency are also rehearsed. The key benefit of using an agency is creativity, knowledge of production capabilities and contacts – their staff are deliberately recruited for one or all of these abilities – and their generation and development of ideas is likely to better than in-house efforts. The importance of establishing the contract at an early stage is covered in the book, which also covers selecting, briefing (which is critical to future success), and paying an agency.

What can they do?

Achieve your marketing communications objectives on the awareness side. Obtain good deals for advertisement placings. Provide quality editorial coverage. Produce valuable research.

The key benefit of employing a 'communications' agency is its innovation and creativity contributions coupled with its technical knowledge of the media with which it works. Its strength lies in the people it employs.

As people are the key resource, should there be a personality clash then you should insist on the removal of the agency person. Otherwise the whole working environment will be affected.

Measuring achievement

If you have set an objective to improve awareness then you need to measure it. The contract should include commission, the necessary measurement. Part of the remuneration might nowadays include an element related to achievement. Carry out a survey before the campaign of marketing activities. Carry out a survey after the campaign. The success or failure should determine the amount you pay and whether you use the agency again.

To measure individual marketing activities see the appropriate sections of the chapters in this part.

To test market research you should check the methodology used by having an observer present on occasion, either openly or covertly.

Inputs from a variety of sources should be consistent – check market research on customers against your own sales staffs' or merchandising staffs' comments on customers.

Desk research may find another firm has carried out similar research. For all market research the objective is usually to allow a decision to be taken. If the research is inconclusive then the agency have advised you poorly on the questions to ask or the nature of the research carried out.

For editorial copy you may need to ascertain that the target print – magazines, newspapers or journals – have been covered and the articles are favourable, in the right place and have the right impact. For TV and radio news coverage similar impact achievement should be set and then assessed. There are organizations that record mentions on radio and visibility on TV.

Achievement mechanisms

Whatever the agency has agreed to do in its contract should be achieved. Measure the cost of marketing activity versus target. Measure the effect on profit.

Consultants

What are they?

Consultants come singly and in small, medium and large firms. The larger the firm and the higher in the organization the more you will pay as a rule of thumb. A track record of what they have achieved for other clients and a referral is a useful guide. You should like and trust any consultant with whom you work. But always check on their actual provenance. (I worked for a 'Fellow' of the Institute of Marketing as it was then, but when the Institute published a list I rang angrily to protest the omission of his name – the omission was not a mistake and the 'Fellow' and I parted company.)

A marketing consultant should be a member of a professional body, have a recognized marketing qualification and nowadays be a 'chartered marketer', which means they undertake ongoing professional training known as continuing professional development (CPD). (A tip on meeting a consultant is to ask what CPD they are undertaking. If the consultant does not know what the letters stand for you should be worried.) In the UK the chartered marketer title is conferred by the Chartered Institute of Marketing. A telephone call will confirm the status of any marketing consultant you are considering using. They can be employed for one-off tasks for a number of days or for, say, a day per month on an ongoing basis.

Consultants should generally come and listen to your problem and, after due consideration, they should be very clear about what they are going to do for you, the result you should expect, and the cost. Effectively you should have a fixed-price contract. The contract should be in writing. They should be fully open about their methodology. I always let clients see questionnaires and let them know all the sources of the material I use.

The use of any consultant(s) brings experience, knowledge and skill to your business. If you do not have a marketing-trained partner or a director with marketing qualifications you should certainly test a consultant to see just what value can be added. I have always tried to demonstrate within a few weeks that the client has made more from the bottom line as a result of employing me than the fees I charge. This is not always possible, say, when evaluating a brand as part of a merger and acquisition exercise, but it is generally possible. If the task is to raise the brand awareness over time, then part of the contract is to measure that. If it is to keep order books full, say for a professional partnership over the year, then a chart or some mutually agreed device may be used to demonstrate that achievement.

What can they do?

A marketing consultant is essential when you are starting up a business and do not have professional marketing talent to call on in your team. Even if your team has marketing talent then be very sure that the advice you are getting is objective. In my experience, sadly, a lot of businesses start off on the wrong market analysis basis – often actually quite unaware of the real feelings of the target market from whom they hope to extract large amounts of cash in purchases of a new concept.

In an existing business you may have learnt the hard way and when you next realize that you have a problem and need advice on a way ahead, by employing a marketing consultant you may well save money, time and lost opportunities compared to if you try to resolve it yourself. Remember any time you spend on the activity is less time that you are able to devote to your normal tasks.

A marketing consultant can carry out desk research knowing precisely where to find and extract the information required. This will be done far more quickly, more reliably and extensively than you can probably achieve on your own. A marketing consultant can carry out small amounts of client research and your clients will say things they may not say to you – using a consultant here is often of double benefit in my experience; clients are intrigued and surprised by the fact that you are employing a marketing consultant and your status goes up if they hear you are using a marketing consultant to carry out client research, while at the same time they actually produce answers for your business. You can use the client comments in the construction of marketing messages; you can resolve faults and errors in the product/service provision; you can rectify misperceptions and find out how strong your brand and the bonds formed with your customers are.

Marketing consultants can help with your strategic issues – which markets to enter and to what extent? Their experience may help you avoid many of the pitfalls touched on in this book.

Measuring achievement

The marketing consultant includes any outputs in the terms of reference of the contract. These outputs should be measurable. Clearly, the contract should state what is to be measured and how that is to be done.

Contract success may be linked to financial reward – but that financial reward will probably be a participatively based figure rather than a fixed sum. Be aware that if consultants are to be rewarded in such a way then they must be allowed to control all the activities fully that are associated with that success. It is not fair on anyone to make their reward depend on the activities of others over whom they have less than absolute control.

Achievement mechanisms

Whatever the contract defines as success is achieved. It is worth seeing if there are side benefits of work carried out by a consultant. One company discovered a highly beneficial direct result of the achievement of high-brand status: it saved the client money on recruitment. High-quality candidates now call asking for employment – even when no jobs are vacant.

Measure the cost of the marketing activity versus the target spend set. Measure the effect on profit.

Advertisements (television commercials and cinema)

What are they?

They are the paid-for advertising placed between programmes that goes towards the cost of operating (commissioning, producing and transmitting) and generating a profit for the commercial TV station.

The commercial itself has to be commissioned, produced and recorded in a legally and commercially acceptable format ready for transmission. It takes about three weeks to clear a commercial through the authorities.

The marketing objective defines the purpose of the commercial. The message, design and format of delivery, length of time, choice of television station and showing of the commercial will be related to the target customer. The length of commercial and the slot(s) occupied will determine the cost to be paid to the television station. Many packages are available for slotting commercials into programmes.

The actual time shooting a simple commercial may only take two days. Much work is required in preparation including drawing up a story board – this is a series of sketches of shots in sequence with the dialogue, effects and music written alongside each frame. Assuming all the preparation is successful then the shoot takes place: days are spent afterwards editing the shot material. In the UK it is often wisest to shoot outdoor scenes indoors, making up a set to the same backdrop required. Delays in shooting awaiting suitable weather windows are very expensive. Still photographs for print material can be taken on the set when shooting is not taking place.

The advent of digital format means that small studios are capable of shooting broadcast-quality commercials.

A spin-off is that if the story board is appropriate or additional filming takes place, it may be possible to make a video out of the shot material.

Throughout the process of making a commercial the marketing objective must be kept to the forefront. It is easy to be swayed as the process moves forward and clever ideas for change occur, to forget the objective. Not always true – on one occasion, while shooting a commercial for Army recruitment, during a break a small scene enacted off set between an Army driver and a German farmer's wife as he negotiated to buy eggs was so appropriate to the objective that it was shot properly and incorporated into the commercial.

Certain commercial television stations consist of nothing but commercials. It is reported that people on average watch for 80 hours before making a purchase.

What can they do?

They can be persuasive for a time and as one of a series of commercials they can be an element of increased awareness and bonding with a brand. One of the BT commercials – 'it's good to talk' – had a positive and measured effect, especially on women – causing them to make calls. But the effect of seeing a television or cinema commercial is transitory. There is no guarantee of uninterrupted transmission on television – it is perhaps better in a cinema where the size of screen, the dark, and focus should allow the massage to be put across.

Viewing figures are available for commercial channels. Cinema groups record ticket purchases.

A cinema commercial can impart a lot of information and make an impact. It certainly can affect attitude. However, the cinema is not a good place in which to take down any information. It is therefore only really beneficial for well-known, existing brands. It is a 'reinforcing and informing' media – this is beneficial where brand bonding is sought.

If an offer is made through a television commercial, then people may respond. The offer may be to send for more information. This usually involves displaying a telephone number, usually of a call centre. Alternatively or in addition a Web site address can be used. These follow-up marketing activities are described elsewhere in this chapter.

Measuring achievement

People who telephone a call centre can be asked where they saw the telephone number. This can give an indication or measure of the success of the advertisement. The same applies to a Web site. The number of hits may and should increase after a commercial screening. The record of hits can be a measure of the success of the advertisement.

Market research will be needed to measure changes in attitude or awareness. Measurement will need to take place both before and after the advertising is screened.

You can measure advertising effectiveness by recall market research. Research on recall is also available for big brands in such magazines as *Campaign*.

Achievement mechanisms

Use market research to measure changes in attitude and awareness. Carry out surveys before and after screenings. Use call centres and Web sites to record the directed response. Measure the cost of marketing activity versus target. Measure the effect on profit.

Advertisements (radio commercials)

What are they?

Radio advertising operates in the same way as television advertising. Interestingly, there are large audiences for radio. Unfortunately the audiences are widely dispersed across many stations, some operating in a really local area, some only seasonally. The local radio stations are worth remembering when you are running an event.

Not all target markets listen to a commercial radio station. Some are purely BBC listeners. (Research has found that accountants listen to Radio 4 rather than anything else, so they are not easy to target via radio.) The transmitter footprint (like a cloverleaf) shows area coverage. A profile of listeners may be available.

Just as for television, a radio commercial has to be produced and cleared before slots can be negotiated. There are 'voice' artists who are available through firms and agencies who will record the commercial. Generally a well-known voice used to making commercials enhances a commercial giving it a professional feel. The use of humour and attention-getting noises (a telephone ringing) needs to be balanced against any irritation caused.

What can they do?

If you have ascertained that your target market listens to radio and you have found the stations it chooses and times that it tunes in, then radio commercials may be for your concept. There are special business programmes.

Particularly useful are morning and evening times when a lot of people are in their cars listening to the radio travelling to and from their place of work. The same is true for parents of children who drive them to school – but only in term times, not holidays or half-terms.

In a short space of time a radio commercial can put across feelings about the concept.

Measuring achievement

The call centre or Web site response can record that people heard about the concept on the radio.

Use market research to measure changes in attitude and awareness. Carry out surveys before and after broadcasts. If the purpose is to sell, record orders.

Achievement mechanisms

Measure the following:

- ■ sales;
- ■ effect on bottom line;
- ■ change in awareness and attitude;
- ■ the cost of marketing activity versus target;
- ■ the effect on profit.

Posters

What are they?

They are normally print material of varying size – usually calculated in the number of sheets – that carries information about your brand, product or service.

Posters are displayed on poster sites. These border major traffic routes – usually at the entry to towns and cities. Sites also border railway lines – particularly where there is a large number of passing trains such as at Clapham Junction.

The use of posters on transport is covered in the transport section below.

What can they do?

They can be very effective for locally targeted customers. It is possible to target the employees of a firm by placing a poster on a site, if available, directly opposite its entrance. If many of your potential customers pass a poster site then it is a very useful means to impart a message. Assuming the poster is eye-catching then it will repeatedly put across your message.

Some of the most famous posters created have been considered to be those used in election campaigns.

Matching site to customers

Invesco has one of the largest poster sites in terms of sheet size adjacent to London Bridge to advertise its financial services to commuters walking across the River Thames to catch trains from their jobs in the City.

Measuring achievement

Poster advertising has mainly sought an awareness or attitude response. There may be some spin-off to sales.

Success may be by an increase in inquiries, even an increase in sales. For awareness or attitude changes you will need market research before and after the display.

Achievement mechanisms
Measure:

■ the cost of marketing activity versus target;
■ the effect on profit;
■ the awareness or attitude improvement through market research;
■ the call centre or Web site response can record that people saw the poster.

Transport (taxi, bus, rail, underground)

What is it?
It is no more than a poster (see above) but one that it is moving or you are moving proceed.

What can it do?

If a wall poster on a platform, or a card inside a bus, train, taxi or tube then, like a normal poster, it can contain wordy messages – albeit in a font size that it is readily readable from the viewing point.

If it is moving or is normally viewed as people walk or travel past then it should contain few words. About six seconds is perhaps the maximum time it will be in view. Few words and clear images are what is required.

To measure the achievement
Transport advertising has traditionally sought a broad range of responses. Some advertising is for awareness or attitude. Some transport advertising is directed towards people taking action, to book tickets, to call a number for further information, to visit an exhibition or show, and so forth. The success of the poster will often be determined by a customer making a call or buying a ticket.

If the poster is for an attraction or to direct people to contact a call centre or Web site then you will need to train people to ask where they saw your message and also to record that fact.

For awareness or attitude changes you will need market research before and after the display.

The early example of the MD of Regus actually relates to the use of escalator poster cards at Underground stations adjacent to the serviced offices. Market research awareness surveys before and afterwards measured the success of the campaign (an increase from 7 to 54 per cent). The improved occupancy/sales rates were another indicator. The bottom line showed improvement. All three measures recorded the success of the marketing activity.

Achievement mechanisms
Measure the awareness or attitude improvement through market research before and after placement. The call centre or Web site response can record that people saw the posters. Measure the cost of marketing activity versus target. Measure the effect on profit.

Directories

What are they?
Traditionally they are a means of entering information about your firm in a printed document that is updated annually. The same print versions are available today but new forms of directory are available such as on CD ROM.

General telephone number directories
The BT telephone directory, often forgotten as a way to market, allows for enhancements such a capital letters, bold type and boxed entries – remember this is part of your corporate image. There are directories such as *Yellow Pages* and *Thomson's* arranged by products and services and covering a geographic area; here size matters, for very large and small text entries are difficult to take in. There are CD-ROM and Web-based directories that contain the same information.

Web site directories
Similar to telephone numbers but using Web sites by product and service category. An example is Seek (0800 169 6820).

Sector, trade, retail, profession directories
There are directories available in print and now on CD ROM and on the Web. These usually give a name as point of contact, with the job title, the name of the company, company address, telephone number, fax and Web site. Such directories often allow a short paragraph describing the company products and services.

Be aware that new types of directories are now being produced – for example for location-based services for use with hand-held devices and those coupled to the latest generation of mobile phones. These new directories are electronic and may be used much more because they are electronic and will be downloaded automatically. They may demand a level of response higher than presently expected as standard.

What can they do?
They target potential customers with your business that you may not otherwise target – particularly those recently entering your location and in need of your product or service. In the case of a specialist concept infrequently supplied to a trade or profession a directory offers a solution to finding a supplier.

A key question is to ascertain that a potential customer is likely to consider using a directory to source your product or service. A business customer is perhaps more likely to search a trade directory rather than a general directory. Some professions, such as solicitor, offering a family service would expect more calls from a *Yellow Pages* or *Thomson* directory; offering a specialist service to commercial firms would be better with an entry into any relevant trade or professional directories. A household tradesman, such as a jobbing builder, would expect to get a large part of work from directory listings. You should include a reference number in the entry (see below).

Internet usage may define the success of the Internet search engines, which operate as directories.

There are now print directories (offline) of Web sites in areas such as central London (www.seekdirectory.co.uk).

Measuring achievement
Practically the benefit of an entry into any directory is probably risky in that whatever is said by the directory publisher it is possible that no one will respond or if they do your staff will forget

to ask or forget to record the fact that the source of an inquiry was the directory. In this respect it is probably worth including in the directory 'please quote reference... when replying' to alert your staff.

Before placing an entry in any directory it is probably worth calling a number of customers to see if they have ever heard of it. What do they think of it? Have they ever used it to source a supplier? It is also probably a good idea to call other suppliers to see if they have found that their entry has generated any business.

Some form of training for your staff – such as sales staff and receptionists – will be needed for those who are tasked to answer persons contacting your firm, to ask where they saw your message and to record that fact. A recording system co-ordinator will need to be appointed to consolidate the measuring of responses. If these actions produce a positive result and business has accrued then all is fine.

Achievement mechanisms
Measure:

■ responses;
■ the cost of marketing activity versus target;
■ the effect on profit.

To put some flesh on how some marketing activities might be put together and the campaign measured as a whole, examples follow.

Part 3

For an existing business – measurement and control for marketing activities

The purpose of this section is to illustrate how to achieve a culture of marketing measurement, measuring every marketing activity in an existing business to show whether you have achieved value for money.

This part of the book deals with an existing business – you have customers who have used your product(s) and service(s); they have purchased your concept. How they value your concept will determine whether they buy from you again and recommend you to others or whether they do not. Often by listening to customers' views you can alter the concept to match their needs: you can spot a trend and seize the opportunities that it provides. Equally, feedback from customers is valuable in promoting to others – potential customers – the messages that you have gained from satisfied customers.

This section sets out notional marketing activities that you might carry out and suggests how you might define and measure the success of each such activity.

The chapters in this section quote a generalized business example. It is not possible to provide specific examples for each kind of business that exists. However the author believes that this generalized marketing solution can be used to confirm the achievement of success of a marketing activity and to illustrate how 'what you need to measure' is determined. The author relies on your imagination to stretch the offering in this section to cover your business.

Chapter 11 is important in that it looks at results. It is important because, however clever the definitions of the key performance indicator and metric, the achievement of success and the measuring mechanisms constructed, it is essential to question both and learn from that questioning.

Measuring marketing activities is a learning process and not only will you learn what marketing activities give you value for money as you repeat the business process, but you will also learn the best key performance indicators and metrics and the best measuring mechanisms to use. What this means is that, although at the end of year one you will have a good idea of the value for money you are getting from marketing activities, it will not be perfect. But it will be far better than before. You will be in control. You will know you have value for money from marketing, from the activities undertaken, from the achievement of objectives and the people in marketing.

8

Drawing together a marketing activities programme

The start point is your business plan for the next period – let's say you are looking at a year ahead. You are, say, in the sports sector, supplying one sport with a range of products to the trade. You have about 400 trade customers.

To use your product successfully consumers need sales staff to give a demonstration and explain how it works. You have developed a 20-minute training session for them or their sales managers to pass on.

You operate a help desk for any use or demonstration queries. There are a number of consumables that your products all use. It is possible to upgrade a product to one higher in the range, so there is a chance for your trade customers to make further sales to consumers.

Let us presume the process in Chapter 2 has been followed for a firm about to start year three of its existence – you have traded for a couple of years. Well done. Remember that the purpose is not to tell you what to do but rather to concentrate on showing you how to set key performance indicators with metrics for success – achievements measuring every marketing activity. This chapter describes the business and suggests a raft of marketing activities that you might select. Chapter 9 looks at the practicality of the selection and trims the activities so you can meet a notional budget; how to control and set key performance indicators for success criteria and measurement mechanisms are detailed in Chapter 10. Chapter 11 runs through to the end of the year and suggests what you might achieve and examines how to make further improvements for the next year. So back to the example.

ILLUSTRATIVE BUSINESS PICTURE

In practice you might just set the business objectives and let the marketing director and marketing managers get on with it thereafter. In particular you would ask the person responsible to define the key performance indicator and metric for success and the measurement mechanism for each marketing activity. Although in practice the tasks described are probably carried out by different people, the process in this section of the book assumes you are operating at all levels.

Let's presume you have understood the need for some strategic marketing input and you commissioned some market research last year. (Have you ever thought of doing that? It is not difficult or costly. Sometimes its findings will immediately bring in money by creating opportunities to make more sales, often bringing in much more than the cost of the research.)

In our notional sports company example, the couple of days' consultancy from a marketing research consultancy gave the following results:

▓ Both the economy and your sector are growing slightly. (You had a gut feeling that this was the case.)
▓ Your niche is described as buoyant, with more new people taking an interest as consumers in the sport and in your concept (products and services). (It is useful to know that for the shareholders.)
▓ The figures for your sports participants and how often people participate, the readership of magazines (lower than you expected) and the viewing figures and screenings of the sports' major activities (much higher than you had appreciated).

■ The figures for sports purchases for all sports is given and the figures for your sport. Interestingly, there are references to the new media and purchases over the Internet and interactive digital TV.

■ Figures for Internet usage, the number of PCs in homes and the growth of interactive TV.

■ Your turnover is not large enough to have a single digit percentage market share in the overall sports market – yet in your niche and for your target markets you are a player in the category in which you sell. A single figure percentage is suggested.

■ Analysis of the lead competitors in your sector show them to be few (you knew that). With one exception they do not compete directly but offer products that produce similar results in a quite different way. (You have accumulated a lot of comments about the direct competitor from journalists and visitors to the exhibitions at which you both had stands.)

The client survey – primary research – carried out on a random sample of 20 trade clients (5 per cent) (actually only 15 were contacted, but the results proved consistent and therefore are reasonably valid) showed that your customers feel that:

■ the product range is 'Rolls Royce';

■ the company has a name that is viewed favourably and the values match the brand that you have been trying to build up, except that there is quite a variation in how well the products sell on to consumers. (The consultant suggests that this may be due to a lack of understanding of the product.);

■ your service is spectacularly good (the same consultant, after year one, made recommendations about improvements to your service – clearly the changes have been successful);

■ about half of your customers have Web sites for their consumers, and Internet access;

■ there is resistance to the price of one product and a suggested price point has been found (you expected that but not an actual figure – worth paying for that information).

The consumer questionnaires sent out by your staff to competition winners at the end of last year find that, although people relate the brand name to the product, they did not know what it did, until they owned one. The products are described as fit to last a lifetime, over-engineered, but they are also described as 'magic', brilliant' and 'a wonder' by consumer purchasers. Again, there are price points offered by some consumers (similar to the consultant research). Many of them watch sport on satellite or cable television. Some buy magazines but often do not have time to read them. They do read newspaper reports about the sport.

The picture of year two's unaudited accounts is given by your financial staff.

An analysis of the previous year's sales figures show a mixed bunch of results compared to the forecast. Some areas are up, some down.

An analysis by product shows far fewer of one product purchased than forecast (you had been aware of this shortfall over the months – many heated discussions on price have taken place).

Feedback from your own sales staff indicates great enthusiasm from people once a real understanding of the product's purpose is achieved. Even your trade customers are still not really sure what the product is for. They report that one product is harder to sell at the current price. (You know which one.)

The call centre used for routing potential customer response from all media towards order-taking outlets (trade customers) reports a fair spread of interest. It has an analysis of the responses generated by each media – both for advertisements and for the editorials generated from your PR activities.

So what do you do? You decide that price and that one product must be investigated at once. You quickly associate the three facts: the product is over-engineered (this gives you scope to reduce the specification); the product has a price point; the product is difficult to sell at the present price. From the price point you work backwards to find the price at which you will need to sell to the trade. You remove a few whistles and bells, but you find you are able to drop a couple of grades of material moving to cheaper materials. You can also simplify the production process by gluing instead of stitching and you reinvent the product colour scheme using only four colours instead of six. Rather surprisingly it looks nicer. Production can now just deliver this basic product at a price that allows you to sell profitably to the trade and allows them to sell on to consumers profitably at the price point. As for the old specification you retain it, putting back all the bells and whistles and you now decide to call it the 'executive' version. You also invent accessory upgrade packs from the basic to the executive. Hurrah. Perhaps you can now achieve or exceed the forecast sales of last year with the new basic product. You decide to set higher targets to make the same profit.

Initial illustrative business objectives

Your business objectives cleared by the board of your company might now be to:

■ sell the existing range of products but with the new basic product which now matches the price point to achieve the target sales figures (which you adjusted upwards to retain the same profit);
■ obtain a higher profile than your direct competitor;
■ take advantage of the new media;
■ launch the revamped product at the category sport exhibition;
■ make people clearly aware of the purpose of your business and the products/service it provides;
■ grow the customer base by 10 per cent (although this figure seems to have been plucked out of the air you base it on production who say this is all the product capacity they can guarantee without buying more machinery).

You then can draw up marketing objectives. These might be be to:

■ achieve the sales targets set including sales of one re-launched product;
■ increase consumer and customer awareness and understanding of the products and their purpose;
■ relaunch the product at the main exhibition;
■ use the new media – Internet and interactive TV;
■ grow the customer database by 10 per cent;
■ maintain the company brand values;
■ raise the profile higher than your direct competitor.

Here you should stop and examine the objectives to see if they meet the SMART criteria – you may be able to live with some but not all of the non-SMART objectives give here. To measure achievement words such as 'clearly aware', 'higher profile' and 'maintain a brand value' are ineffectual.

Illustrative promotional marketing activity
What, then, are the promotional marketing activities that might result? Some thinking produces the following result:

■ There is a need for further marketing to improve brand aware-ness, and a lot of education to increase understanding, which in itself should help sales – after all you have 400 trade customers. Marketing activities that could be undertaken are demonstra-tions at the sport's sporting clubs and at the main and other exhibitions or at customer locations (you decide to do all three). These are opportunities for you to feed in the brand values as well and obtain PR coverage and put out press releases.

■ You decide to go for more PR than advertising and to concen-trate on newspapers rather than magazines, based on the consumer survey, but you will look at interactive TV – the consultant is persuasive and the board has set it as an objective. The saving on print-based advertising could be considerable and you will put this into these new media activities.

■ You will need a TV commercial and out of this can come a video to demonstrate the products. From the TV commercial you will link replies to the call. Just launching the video can be an event. The trade press might be particularly interested and potential customers can be sent one.

■ The Web site (the company has resisted this to date but it is part of the new media the board is keen to try) could be an alterna-tive or an additional response mechanism from just using the call centre. (The market research from the consultant has pointed to some research findings on what makes a Web site interesting, so that people return to the site again and again, because this leads to purchases. He has also fed in the need to provide reasonable resources on a ratio of 1: 2: 5 for develop-ment: maintenance: operation.) Your Web site would be for consumers, principally directing them to your trade customers. You decide to make the Web site interesting by including a game based on your concept on the Web site – the game para-meters changing weekly – with a reward for the top scorer each week.

- Direct mail for specific targets, because it is proving fairly difficult to put across what the products achieve. (OK, you are good at mailshots.) You might e-mail potential customers and direct them to the Web site or to an exhibition or demonstration, or send them a video.
- E-mail could be a way of contacting some existing customers, the ones already on the Internet perhaps – directing them to the Web site, taking orders (You decide to explore this – you have heard it can save costs. You may try to do this with an extranet.)
- What about obtaining editorials in newspapers and magazines? This can be achieved using PR and PR agencies. (You have decided in the light of the research to dispense with the magazine advertising but to go for PR – you could invite journalists to the demonstrations or exhibitions – send them a copy of the video.)
- You could sponsor a competition, or more than one – they must be the right kind of events and fairly risk free so that your brand is likely to be enhanced. (You decide to investigate.)
- There is an opportunity to relaunch the basic product at the new price. You could also launch the video and the Web site. You decide to explore the opportunity for launches as part of the other marketing activities (see above); the relaunch is to be at the main exhibition.
- Growing the customer database is probably best achieved by direct marketing inviting the prospects to the marketing activities (see above). You decide to make follow-up telephone calls as well.
- Marketing training and support (something you will need to explore further) both for your own staff and those of your customers.
- Finally there is the main exhibition itself with which a whole raft of marketing activities will be associated. But the exhibition is late in the year, which is a pity as you could otherwise use it for the product relaunch. But that is a board business objective – it may not work...

There are probably enough illustrative marketing activities for our purpose – to illustrate setting up the measurement process. You may need to examine whether they offer enough flair and excitement to be different from the rest.

A check with the marketing objectives will show that the marketing activities list above – though seemingly pretty inclusive – has actually missed some things out. For example, little is done to support directly the achievement of the sales targets set or the 10 per cent increase in customers. Nothing supports the achievement of a higher profile over the competitor. One business objective, which was to relaunch the product at the category exhibition, is unachievable. This cannot be done or the penalty will be to delay sales. You return to the board and explain – they agree. The relaunch moves to the first demonstration. But the purpose of the main exhibition now becomes questionable – unless it is included in a plan for next year. It may now be irrelevant to this year – but see below. The board also agree to sharpen up the business objectives.

Final business objectives

The final SMART (S = Specific, M = Measurable, A = Agreed, R = Reasonable, T = Timebound) business objectives of your company, cleared by the board in a priority order, might now be to:

■ sell the existing range of products, with the new revamped basic product, to achieve the target sales (a figure in pounds sterling is included here) within the calendar year;
■ grow the customer base by 10 per cent, that is 40 new long-term customers by the end of the year;
■ be established in the new media with interactive television and a Web site operating in the next six months;
■ achieve a profile at the end of the year that places the perception and image of this firm and its products above your direct competitor (list of attributes, benefits, features to be agreed by end January);
■ take a stand at the main sport exhibition;
■ raise the awareness to 80 per cent by the end of the year among those that play, spectate or train in the sport of the purpose of your business and the concept – products/services – it provides.

You draw up amended marketing objectives again in a priority order. These might be to:

■ achieve the sales targets set for the year;

- grow the customer database by 40 long-term customers by the end of this year;
- install the new media – Internet and interactive television – within six months;
- raise the profile (using an agreed list of measures) to be higher at the end of the year than your direct competitor;
- operate a stand at the main exhibition;
- increase awareness of the purpose of the firm and understanding of the products/services for those active in the sport to above 80 per cent.

Promotional marketing activities
The new list, with marketing activities relisted by marketing objectives, shows more clearly than the previous list where additional marketing activities are required.

To achieve the sales targets set for the year
Mailshots to customers:

- at start of year – what is happening – product relaunch, demonstrations, Web site, main exhibition, interactive television, video, prizes for local newspaper competitions;
- invitations to demonstrations, training sessions for customer staff;
- offering sales promotions to customers at demonstrations;
- offering sales promotions for consumers;
- for video launch;
- for Web site launch – extranet enrolment;
- feedback on interactive television and Web site take-up;
- following up some mailshots with telemarketing;
- repeat mailshots after telemarketing as required;
- offering extranet ordering;
- offering customers sales promotions for extranet-placed orders both as one-offs and as a general policy (passing on order administration cost saving?);
- directing people to the Web site to place orders on your customers;
- directing people through a call centre to your nearest customer;
- inviting people to the main exhibition (extend invitation to selected consumers through customer).

To grow the customer database by 40 long-term customers by the end of this year

Mailshots to potential customers:

■ invitation to become a customer – product relaunch, demonstrations, Web site, main exhibition, interactive TV, video, prizes for local newspaper competitions;
■ invitation to demonstrations;
■ send a video;
■ refer to Web site launch;
■ invite to main exhibition;
■ feedback on quarterly performance of sales, Web, interactive television, extranet ordering;
■ follow up all mailshots with telemarketing.

To install the new media – Internet and interactive TV – within six months
Producing a (50 per cent repeat-visited) Web site (interactive television operable) development:

■ maintenance – plus game parameters change weekly;
■ operation;
■ Web site allowing customers to order through an extranet used by all Internet user customers.

Television commercials (and videos) resulting from television shoots showing on interactive TV probably during a major event involving the sport. The interactive part would direct people to the Web site and call centre to place orders.

To raise the profile (using an agreed list of measures) to be higher at the end of the year than your direct competitor
■ High visibility creative event at main exhibition;
■ Organize related PR.
■ The drip-feed of marketing activities, particularly using PR, should help raise the company's profile.

To operate a stand at the main exhibition
Organize stand, manning, administration, promotion, PR (general for press/media not on our list – press packs, and so forth).

To increase consumer and customer awareness and understanding of the products and their purpose
■ Demonstrations at customer locations, sports clubs, other exhibitions.
■ PR. Press releases – telephone calls – newspapers, magazines for demonstrations.
■ Visits to newspaper offices (near demonstrations to demonstrate concept).
■ Product relaunch.
■ Video.
■ Web site.
■ Interactive television.
■ Main exhibition (see above).
■ Sponsor competition.
■ Television commercial (producing videos as an offshoot) and showing on interactive television probably during a major event involving the sport.
■ Launch of the video (consumers through trade customers invited to send for one).
■ Web site launch.
■ The main exhibition as finale for the year.
■ The fulfilment, call centre and market research activity.
■ Marketing training and support (something you will need to explore further) both for your own staff and those of your customers.

Non-promotional marketing activities
You have spent some time sorting out the promotional marketing activities:

In-house staff
■ Your own staff includes a marketing director and two managers each with a staff of two or three.
■ You have a Sales staff of four for order taking/order processing, manning a customer hotline.
■ You plan a training day. You will have such training days on an ongoing basis.
■ Your staff will need you to set work objectives after they have agreed the marketing activities, the criteria of success and the measuring mechanisms. This is done through the IiP appraisal system.

Outsourced staff
- Call centre.
- Staff training.
- Telemarketing team.
- Script briefing.

Corporate branding
Time to look at the logo, corporate style, headed paper, and so forth. It is three years since anyone reviewed the brand. The company brand needs to be policed with customers.

New product development
You will need to put some time into product development – this may require a market research activity. You will put a questionnaire in with the relaunched product and see what response you get. Checking marketing activities against the marketing objectives changed the programme of activities. It seems easier to start with SMART marketing objectives and then think through the marketing activities needed for each one – the focus and balance is then correctly placed.

The marketing activities programme may still be too ambitious when costed – it may need to be trimmed in the light of the cost (see Chapter 6). You then need to set the measurement of the achievement of success criteria and the mechanisms to measure each marketing activity (see Chapter 7).

Examples of market research on clients and customers providing benefit greater than the cost of the research

Professional partnership
A company paid for two days of research of their own clients. When asking about the services provided, two clients reported to the researcher that they wanted to pay bills but no invoices had been raised. This seeming error had resulted from a misunderstanding of an instruction of which the company's partners were not aware. Invoices were raised; cash flowed in. From the same survey several former clients were reminded of the existence of the company and offers to pitch for work poured in. The successful settlement of the invoices resulted in more

money than the client paid for the research. The market research opportunities to pitch for contracts was a side benefit to the findings – that clients felt that once a contract was completed they were forgotten about (which was of course true). A contact programme was then put in place at two levels to keep the company in the mind of the people within its own clients' firms and to remove the problem in future. The market research has been repeated twice at 18-month intervals since.

Manufacturer
Another client funded two days of research and the researcher here found unhappiness with the finished product. A quick investigation found that the packers had changed their methods of packing and a new courier firm was less than careful. The cost of replacing damaged stock was stopped, saving more than the cost of the research. A repeat of the research extracted ideas for new product lines, which subsequently proved popular. A major finding was that the brand image and perceptions were confirmed (the descriptions of the manufacturer given to the researcher matched the brand value image; in fact the reality is quite different). Reactions to price increases were obtained, proving the acceptance and acceptability of the price increases and the way they were introduced.

9

Ring-fencing: Putting the Figures In

Rearranging the marketing activities into single responsibility groupings will make the marketing activities easier to give as responsibilities.

Marketing director:
- Overall responsibility for all promotional marketing objectives.
- Direct responsibility for the IiP appraisal system for all marketing staff.
- Overall responsibility for outsourcing contracts.
- New product development.
- Questionnaire with the relaunched product.
- Corporate branding, policing and review.
- Marketing training and support for your own staff.

Manager A marketing activities:
To achieve the sales targets set for the year:

- Mailshots to customers.
- Telemarketing – briefing.
- Extranet ordering.
- Extranet offers.

To grow the customer database by 40 long-term customers by the end of this year:

Mailshots to potential customers; telemarketing.

To increase consumer and customer awareness and understanding of the products and their purpose:

■ Demonstrations – organize and run.
■ PR (agency?) – oversee.
■ Launch of the video.
■ Web site launch.
■ Non-promotional marketing activities.
■ A response and fulfilment campaign (including videos).
■ Call centre – training.
■ Editorial competition fulfilment.
■ Telemarketing follow-up to direct mailings to invite to exhibitions, demonstrations market research – both for measurement and NPD (see next chapter).

Manager B marketing activities:
To install the new media – Internet and interactive TV – within six months:

■ Producing a (50 per cent repeat-visited) Web site (interactive TV operable) with extranet.
■ Development.
■ Maintenance – plus game parameters change weekly.
■ Operation.
■ Television commercial (and video) brief, shooting, production resulting showing on interactive television slots.

To raise the profile (using an agreed list of measures) to be higher at the end of the year than that of your direct competitor:

■ High visibility creative event at main exhibition.
■ Organize related PR.

To operate a stand at the main exhibition:

Organize stand, manning, administration, promotion, PR (general for press/media not on our list – press packs, and so forth).

You are aware that there will be further marketing activities measurement activities to follow, resulting from the measurement of all of the above, which will incur cost, but you are committed to measure marketing to see if you achieve value. In reality it is important to let the managers set what their achievement of success is going to be and then decide how that is to be measured. The measuring mechanism can be overseen by the accountant. These mechanisms will become clearer later.

COSTING THE MARKETING ACTIVITIES

This book is about marketing measurement, not costs directly, so although a costing exercise could prove valuable – and please feel free to go ahead and cost the marketing activities – this book is not going to deal with this here.

For illustration purposes lets say the cost is found to be too much. Basic pruning needs to be carried out: instant savings can be made removing the glitter – the gloss.

The 'celebrity' is cut from the television commercial and replaced with a sports professional who is quite well known and supports the product. This makes a significant saving as the shooting takes a couple of days and is weather dependent. The 'celebrity' would have had to be paid for all the days.

An examination of the demonstration places – sporting clubs/other exhibition venues and customer outlets across the UK – allows a reduction to about 10 sites from an original 30-plus possibilities while still giving reasonable cover. It means that the team will be on site two or three days to accommodate the number of customers staff, your own staff, and invited consumers, but can still give the training and relaunch briefing on the basic product in either half a morning or half an afternoon (four sessions a day). The press will be invited locally with the national newspapers' sports writers and sports magazines invited to the first one – at a sporting club or other exhibition (that still has to be fixed). This whole programme will take three months (from February).

You decide to remove the idea of a nationally sponsored competition – expensive and difficult to arrange – but you will offer, as part of a PR campaign, a free product to the winner of newspaper competitions, if an editor agrees. Although you will invite the editors and journalists to demonstrations, they rarely attend, so you decide to arrange for someone to visit them with the basic product where possible. This will surprise them. The visits can be tagged onto the 10 site demonstrations. The costs of the competition concept prizes must be added in – you wonder about the best way to make the awards. You decide that a local customer and a local journalist will present them.

You never get all that you want even when you prune drastically; how to protect the core is what matters. But actually we have not looked at the core – the marketing objectives.

A recheck of costs indicates that the figures are still over budget. You decide to look at measurement and then prune some more.

But are the marketing objectives really covered? What will be our criteria of success? Can everything be measured? See the next chapter!

10

Control and measure the operation

Ring-fencing is important in order to make control easier. The rough grouping of marketing activities by managers in Chapter 9 appeared to do this satisfactorily. You check the delegation and ownership of marketing activities at lower levels than your managers. The next stage is to cost the marketing activities and total to see if they are over or under budget. You need some leeway to allow for the cost of measuring the marketing activities. Remove the gilt but retain the core.

The next task is to decide what is to be the successful achievement of each marketing activity to set the key performance indicator and its metric.

The actual defining of the success of any activity is what you decide it is to be. It may well ultimately be the bottom-line contribution – the contribution of that marketing activity to the net profit – but it is not always so. The reason is that, in the short term of any one year, some measures cannot be applied reasonably.

For example, take the marketing objective 'to achieve 40 new customers'. The point is made that the 40 new customers will have been recruited over the whole year and not just all in the first month. You may have been able to assess the 40 customers found early on in the year as matching the existing customers by their placing of orders and other repeat business. But the new customers coming along right at the end of the year will have hardly had time to place more than one order. You have no bottom-line indication, at this stage, that the latest recruits are new customers with the ordering potential of long-term customers. Who knows? In the last few weeks of the year you may, by chance, have recruited people that only place one order. That is, they are not going to become long-term customers. Therefore 'orders taken or a pattern of ordering' as a measure to confirm that you have found long-term customers is only an effective measure over the long term; it cannot reasonably be applied to recently recruited new customers found near the end of the year.

An alternative measuring mechanism needs to be found to show that you have recruited long-term customers. The measure needs to be applicable in the short term. For example, a measuring mechanism that might be applied is to show that each new customer matches the profile of existing customers. This can be found, even in the short term, by requiring new customers to answer questions and by verifying facts and status, which give an indication that they match the profile of long-term customers. You will, of course, have to know the profile of your long-term customers first – another measurement.

Another example of the problem of the definition of success is the success, say, of a Web site. The number of hits on a Web site is not an indication of the success of a Web site. A 'hit' in any case can be made numerous times by a single person on a single visit – depending on how a 'hit' has been defined (sometimes every time a different part of a Web site is clicked on can be recorded as a 'hit'). A hit may be an indication of the success of an advertisement elsewhere that has led people to the Web site, particularly if you are measuring whether the 'hits' are made by different people. A better indication of a Web site success is repeat visits to it or activities such as registration. An even finer indication of success might be the placing of orders – for example, on the Web site. Repeat orders are even better; so the earlier but finer single purchase indication is no longer ultimate – you now have a clear match with existing customers. The intermediate stages are possibly good pointers.

Chapters 3 to 7 covered marketing activities. In each case the marketing activity was described in some detail, an indication of what the marketing activity can do was given, measures of success that are appropriate were recorded and then some measuring mechanisms to apply were stated.

Chapters 3 to 7 did not include every marketing activity; you may use others, particularly with new technology. But the principle of measuring every marketing activity still applies. And in order to know what to measure you need to define the success of each marketing activity.

To help with the definition of 'success' Chapters 3 to 7 gave ideas and clues as to what success might be. The selection of the definition of success is yours. You set the key performance indicator and its metric. The marketing activity must give you 'value for money'. This requires you to make a subjective judgement. That is why this book cannot define success for you but can only give an indication. Subjective judgement applies when you value the cost of each marketing activity in terms of what it has achieved. Your subjective view of the success of a marketing activity may be changed subsequently in the light of experience.

Remember that the example in this chapter is looking at all levels – you are taking on the persona of CEO, marketing director, manager and staff. The book suggests you let the person responsible for the marketing activity be the person who makes the decision on defining what is success. That person has argued for their allocation of budget for that marketing activity. You have required them also to include the cost of measuring that activity in the budget. You have presumably also agreed that budget. The marketing activity achievement of success has been set as a work objective for that person. That person will be appraised at the end of the year on the success of the marketing activity. If everything goes well, fine. If everything goes wrong then everyone has learnt in the light of experience and a different but mutually acceptable definition of success (set against the cost determination) will be the new subjective value-for-money achievement of that marketing activity in future.

Measuring value-for-money marketing is a refining discipline – it is a new culture – but eventually the process of measuring all marketing activities will result in everyone knowing what is value for money in marketing. The process developed by accountants to define success in the handling of money is still being refined and will continue. The same applies to value-for-money marketing. Initially your process will be unrefined, but after only a few cycles of the business process you will find better definitions of success and, more importantly, you and others around you will know what is value-for-money marketing.

Measuring the success you have defined requires care. The application of ingenuity may work wonders. Measuring mechanisms may be simple one-off measurements – such as a sales figure. Measuring mechanisms may need to be set as a duo – that is measuring before and after a marketing activity. A measuring mechanism may need to be in the form of a tracking device – recording a trend over a period of time. The frequency of measurement has then also to be considered.

As an inherent common-sense measure, the person responsible for a marketing activity and defining success should not be the person operating the measuring mechanism.

For control purposes, and sometimes decision taking, you may require the measurements to be fed back more than just at the end of the marketing activity. Examples are where an early indication of a trend would allow you to make a decision to change a marketing activity (for example whether to change one advertisement or commercial with another depending on audience reaction), or when you have a foreboding and you wish to reduce risk exposure (for example when you feel possibly no sales may be achieved for a new concept and indeed when no sales are achieved and you wish to cease further promotion).

EXAMPLE IN TABLE FORMAT

Table 10.1 gives success measures and mechanisms for measuring the marketing activities covered in the example in this chapter.

Note that the marketing objectives have also been included for measurement in the table. This allows the relative contributions of marketing activities to be taken into account. It is useful for comparisons of value-for-money of each marketing activity against each other.

The table is purely illustrative and, of course, in different businesses the definition of 'success' and the mechanisms to measure it might be quite different.

The table shows a costs column for illustrative purposes. That

Table 10.1 *Measuring success and the mechanisms with which to measure marketing activities*

Marketing activity	What is success? The key performance indicator and its metric	Measurement mechanism	Cost of activity and measure	Value for money achieved	Mechanism works?	Future use of activity/ mechanism
Marketing objectives: To achieve the sales targets set for the year	Achieve the £ figure set	Sales figures – by month, by area, by customer, for year				
To grow the customer database by 40 long-term customers by the end of this year	40 new customers matching the profile of existing customers	Customer database figures – check match of new with old (completed questionnaire, verify and status checks)				
To install the new media – Internet and interactive TV – within six months	Successfully installed Web site and TV commercial made – interactive TV time booked	Observation				
To raise the profile (using an agreed list of measures) to be higher at the end of the year than your direct competitor	Profile is higher on all measures listed (list agreed by board) Measure mid-year to check on position as well as year end	Check recent market research, if not suited recommission. Market research at middle and end of year after the exhibition				
To operate a stand at the main exhibition	Presence to support profile achievement. Budget yet to be agreed	Observation. Scope for high-visibility activity				
To increase awareness to above 80%, for those active in the sport, of the purpose of the firm and understanding of the products/services	>80% of those questioned respond favourably Questionnaire to be agreed with the board	Market research after the exhibition – combine with profile-raising research				

Table 10.1 (continued)

Marketing activities

Mailshots to customers and potential customers	3% response from potential customers (telemarket anyone not responding – see next activity)	Coded responses allow tracking – record totals of mailshots and telemarketing						
Telemarketing potential customers and customers	10% responses from potential customers (including mailshot)	Use call logs plus customer database record						
Extranet ordering	Ordering by all Web-enabled customers	Compare database of e-mail customers with orders						
Extranet sales promotions	Sales growth with profit >promotion cost and by all Web-enabled customers	Track responses and orders/offer taken up c.f. database						
Web site ordering by consumers	Shows growth across all areas (persuades non e-mail customers to go on Web)	Track order placing through to customer link						
Call centre ordering by consumers	Shows growth across all areas	Call centre log, track coded responses to customers						
Main exhibition acceptances from potential customers	10% response and attend (nil responses telemarketing)	Track coded responses						
Produce a Web site	With 50% repeat visitors	Track site visitors, record repeat visitors						
High-visibility activity at main exhibition	An exhibition stopper Budget figure: negotiate nearer time	Observation						

Table 10.1 (continued)

Marketing activity	What is success? The key performance indicator and its metric	Measurement mechanism	Cost of activity and measure	Value for money achieved	Mechanism works?	Future use of activity mechanism
PR for high-visibility activity	Coverage in a number of national newspapers, articles by commentators and sports journalists in magazines and local papers, radio and TV sports?	Measure see/display rate equivalent Breadth of coverage Impact of activity: use market research				
Main exhibition organize	Stand is favourably commented on. Budget figure: negotiate nearer time	Observation				
Main exhibition PR	See PR for high visibility – above	Measure see/display rate equivalent				
Demonstrations (10 off)	Attendance to 80% capacity of demonstrations with at least 100 potential customers overall, all staff trained	Record visitor number by category; staff, customers, potential customers, press, consumers				
PR – (agency?) programme	Each element obtains coverage greater than cost × 4	Measure see/display rate equivalent				
TV commercial produce	Within budget, to time	Observation Accountant's figures				
TV commercial show	Five-figure response rate in total from Web site and call centre. Rated better than competitors commercials	Measure call centre and Web site activity Market research before and after				

Table 10.1 (continued)

Interactive TV slots	Adjacent to sports major fixtures, within budget	Observation Accountant's figures			
Web site produce	To time and cost within budget	Observation Accountant's figures			
Web site launch	A five-figure number of visitors within a month, excluding repeats	Measurement built into site			
Video produce	To time and cost, within budget	Observation Accountant's figures			
Video launch	Comment in the press greater than cost of launch Rated well by customers and consumers	Measure see/display rate equivalent. Market research afterwards (sample only)			
Extranet produce	To time and cost within budget	Observation Accountant's figures			
Marketing training	All staff trained	Training records – feedback to confirm			
Marketing staff appraisals	All staff work objectives set; finally all appraised	Personnel records – feedback to confirm			
Call centre	Performs to contract	Checks			
Fulfilment – outsourced	Performs to contract	Checks			
Telemarketing	Performs to contract	Checks			
Market research – outsourced	Performs to contract	Checks			

Table 10.1 (continued)

Marketing activity	What is success? The key performance indicator and its metric	Measurement mechanism	Cost of activity and measure	Value for money achieved	Mechanism works?	Future use of activity/ mechanism
Market research – in-house	Attitudes/awareness found or trend recorded. Satisfactory measurement when used as a mechanism	Produce answers – information for decision taking				
Outsource contracts	To time and cost within budget. Meet the brief	Observation Accountant's figures				
New product development	Attitudes/awareness found or trend recorded	Produce answers – information for decision taking				
Relaunch product questionnaire	To save time as relaunch. Ideal response to be at 200 per week. Useful comments resulting	Observation. Record response quantity and quality. Comments found to be positively useful				
Corporate branding review (complete two months before main exhibition)	Satisfactory completion mid-year. Allows rectification at main exhibition possibility	Receive report and recommendations by mid-year				
Brand policing	No transgressions reported	Observation				

column is not completed here. Other columns are for evaluation later – at the end of the year.

Once the definitions of 'success' are confirmed and the measurement mechanisms decided, the costing exercise can be completed. Each measuring mechanism is costed and the cost added to the marketing activity. At this point it may be necessary to prune activities or to seek extra funding to cover the cost.

Once the programme of marketing activities is accepted and cleared by the board (as part of the annual business process of review) then the programme can be implemented.

The final part is to consider the outcomes to find out whether you have value-for-money marketing.

Control and obtaining value for money

Each marketing activity has a defined measure of success – a key performance indicator with a metric. You have a measuring mechanism operating to record the achievement. You compare the measured achievement against the defined measure of success – the key performance indicator metric. Is it value-for-money marketing?

There are two further considerations. The actual validity of the measurement method should be considered both in terms of performance and relative cost. Excessive measurement costs may not be acceptable just as it would probably be unacceptable for the cost of the marketing activity to exceed the budget.

Assess the value of knowing the result against not knowing anything.

Evaluate the future use of the marketing activity when considering its contribution to meeting objectives. Should the marketing activity be used again as it is, or modified, or not used again at all? Any changes that might be made to the measurement mechanism should be noted.

The chosen definition of success of the marketing activity – the key performance indicator metric – is compared with the measured outcome.

There are probably five alternative outcomes to consider:

- Did the result vastly exceed the success definition?
- Did the result meet the success definition – proving value-for-money marketing?
- Did the result not quite meet the success definition?
- Did the result only partially meet the success definition?
- Did the result fail completely, with no indication at all of success?

Did the result vastly exceed the success definition?

Value-for-money marketing – certainly. Next time the definition of success might well be altered to accommodate this result. Check that there was no extraneous reason for success being exceeded so well. The reason may just be that the person responsible was predicting a cautious outcome in their own interest. Such staff should be encouraged and assisted to be bolder next time and confident in their own talent.

Did the result meet the chosen success definition?

Value-for-money marketing – certainly. Again, check that there was no extraneous reason for success. If the result is exactly as predicted there may be a reason for such perfection – it is probably statistically unusual to exactly achieve a prediction. Some manipulation of outcomes may have occurred.

Did the result not quite meet the success definition?

The result should be checked to see whether a day or a week would have made a difference. Sometimes an absolute measurement such as the end of an accounting period may cause an order to be missed because, although an order had been received, it had not been processed. If there are no mitigating circumstances then the result should be accepted as it is but investigated to understand why success was not quite achieved.

Did the result only partially meet the success definition?

When success is a long way off then an investigation to understand why should examine the marketing activity's effectiveness. For example, if a contributory marketing activity was a mailshot was it not understood (although a mailshot should always be tested first); this could be checked with a sample – say making a few calls to recipients – to ask for their comments.

Did the result fail completely?

Clearly something went very wrong. The marketing activity was ill-chosen for the target market. The target market could be checked with a sample – say by making a few calls to the target market. It is just possible that the mechanism was inappropriate for the measuring task, although if due process had been followed the mechanism is unlikely to be that wrong. If the target market is found to not respond to the marketing activity, this is a fault of the person deciding to use the marketing activity.

The measuring mechanism

There are the following considerations:

■ Did the mechanism work in the way expected?
■ Did the mechanism operate fairly and was it not/could it not be fiddled?
■ How much did it cost and is this acceptable in relation to the marketing activity cost?

A positive evaluation of the above will give encouragement to use the mechanism in the future. If the mechanism worked and was fair but relatively expensive, then that should be taken into account in the future. Perhaps a cheaper alternative could be sought or, if it is a market research mechanism, reducing the sample size but returning to the original sample size as a fallback if that sample is producing inconsistent outcomes.

Example result

Table 11.1 illustrates what the outcome might have been. The story presented by the table suggests that the sales target and customer growth marketing objectives were met but that high sales in some areas masked poor performance elsewhere. The Web site and interactive TV were obviously problematic and Web results are below expectation. The high-profile event carried the main exhibition, which also helped achieve the higher profile over the direct competitor marketing objective. Awareness of the firm and its products could be improved.

The combination of mailshot and telemarketing worked but not the mailshot on its own. The extranet ordering took off, but the Web site itself does not seem to be producing the result. Time to get in an expert? The Web site person in marketing manager B's team may not be suited and manager B should have spotted the shortfall. The appraisals should probe this in some depth. The demonstrations were heavy going and some lessons may need to be learnt. The corporate brand activities also need a push – the mechanisms were ineffective and more thought needs to be given here, perhaps also to motivate and produce interest.

Weighting of the result

In the example, the achievement of sales targets and 40 new customers was placed equally alongside the other achievements; in reality these achievements might be overshadowed by the success of the high-profile event. Ironically the market leadership provided by the high-profile event will probably help sales and customer growth next year more than marketing activities directly in support. Perhaps next year a new business objective should be to retain market leadership.

Next year

It is now possible to start thinking of next year repeating the cycle started in Chapter 8.

The process of measuring marketing activities has certainly meant that all marketing activities have been looked at and a value judgement made. In this example you might well be able to consider that, overall, you have achieved value-for-money marketing.

Table 11.1 *Success achievement and analysis – example*

Marketing activity	What is success? The key performance indicator and its metric	Measurement mechanism	Cost of activity and measure	Value for money Achieved	Mechanism works	Future use of activity mechanism
Marketing objectives:						
To achieve the sales targets set for the year	Achieve the £ figure set	Sales figure – by month, by area, by customer, for year	OK	Yes, overall	Yes	Split target by area – some poor
To grow the customer database by 40 long-term customers by the end of this year	40 new customers matching the profile of existing customers	Customer database figures – check match of new with old (completed questionnaire, verify and status checks)	OK	Yes 60 new customers	Yes Profile needs better definition	Use
To install the new media – Internet and interactive TV – within six months	Successfully installed web site and TV commercial made – interactive TV – time booked	Observation	Both Web and ITV cost more	Uncertain	Yes	
To raise the profile (using an agreed list of measures) to be higher at the end of the year than your direct competitor	Profile is higher on all measures listed (list agreed by board) Measure mid-year to check on position as well as year end	Check recent market research, if not suited recommission. Market research at mid- and end of year after the exhibition	Above budget	Yes, even though over	Yes	Enthusiastic – benefit of becoming market leader
To operate a stand at the main exhibiton	Presence to support profile achievement Budget yet to be agreed	Observation. Scope for high visibility activity	Accepted by board	See panel above		
To increase awareness to above 80%, for those active in the sport, of the	>80% of those questioned respond favourably Questionnaire to be	Market research after the exhibition – combine with profile raising	OK	Yes, despite 73%	Yes	Essential

purpose of the firm and understanding of the products/services	agreed with the board	research		Useful to know		
Mailshots to customers and potential customers	3% response from potential customers (telemarket anyone not responding – see next activity)	Coded responses allow tracking – record totals of mailshots and telemarketing	OK	Not mail shot on its own	Yes, early problems recording	Yes
Telemarketing potential customers and customers	10% responses from potential customers (including mailshot)	Use call logs plus customer database record	OK, combined	Yes	Yes	Yes
Extranet ordering	Ordering by all Web-enabled customers	Compare database of e-mail customers with orders	OK	Yes – taken off	Yes	Certainly
Extranet sales promotions	Sales growth with profit >promotion cost and by all Web-enabled customers	Track responses and orders/offer taken up of database	OK	Brilliant	Yes	Yes
Web site ordering by customers	Shows growth across all areas (persuades non e-mail customers to go on Web)	Track order placing through to customer link	OK	Not yet	Yes	Persist
Call centre ordering by consumers	Shows growth across all areas	Call call centre, track coded responses to customers	OK	Yes	Yes	Yes
Main exhibition acceptances from potential customers	10% response and attend (nil responses telemarketing)	Track coded responses				
Produce a Web site	With 50% repeat visitors	Track site visitors, record repeat visitors	More expensive	No – not enough repeats	Yes	Need to make site more exciting with more promotion

Table 11.1 (continued)

Marketing activity	What is success? The key performance indicator and its metric	Measurement mechanism	Cost of activity and measure	Value for Money Achieved	Mechanism works	Future use of activity/ mechanism
High-visibility activity at main exhibition	An exhibition stopper Budget figure: negotiate nearer time	Observation	Board agreed	Yes	Not a proper test	Use a more scientific means
PR for high-visibility activity	Coverage in a number of national newspapers, articles by commentators and sports journalists in magazines and local papers, radio and TV sports?	Measure see/display rate equivalent. Breadth of coverage. Impact of activity: use market research	Board agreed	Worked	Fantastic	Well worthwhile
Main exhibition organize	Stand is favourably commented on. Budget figure: negotiate nearer time	Observation	Board agreed	Board happy		Without high profile might reason
Main exhibition PR	See PR for high visibility – above	Measure see/display rate equivalent	Board agreed	As for high profile	As for high profile	
Demonstrations (10 off)	Attendance to 80% capacity of demonstrations with at least 100 potential customers overall, all staff trained	Record visitor number by category; staff, customers, potential customers, press, consumers	Over budget	Hard work to fill to 70%	Hard work to record	Yes, lessons valuable
PR – (agency?) programme	Each element obtains coverage greater than cost ×4	Measure see/display rate equivalent	OK	Yes, much more	Yes, but raise to ×7	See if there is a better mechanism
TV commercial produce	Within budget, to time	Observation. Accountant's figures	Over	Unsure	Measure needs to	Feel could have had

					look at outcome	same for less
TV commercial show	Five-figure response rate in total from Web site and call centre. Rated better than competitors commercials	Measure call centre and Web site activity. Market research before and after	OK	No, over-ambitious on Web	Yes	Rating OK, much less than target
Interactive TV slots	Adjacent to sports major fixtures, within budget	Observation. Accountant's figures	OK	Yes	Yes	
Web site produce	To time and cost, within budget	Observation. Accountant's figures	OK	No	No – measure outcomes	Should have tied in with outcomes – poor
Web site launch	A five-figure number of visitors within a month, excluding repeats	Measurement built into site	OK	No	Yes	
Video produce	To time and cost, within budget	Observation. Accountant's figures	OK	Yes	Yes	
Video launch	Comment in the press greater than cost of launch. Rated well by customers and consumers	Measure see/display rate equivalent. Market research afterwards (sample only)	Just below	Not far off	Yes	Yes
Extranet produce	To time and cost, within budget	Observation. Accountant's figures	OK	Yes, good result	Yes	Yes
Marketing training	All staff trained	Training records – feedback to confirm	OK	Yes	Yes	Yes
Marketing staff appraisals	All staff work objectives set; finally all appraised	Personnel records – feedback to confirm	OK	Yes	Yes	Powerful! Web person out!

Table 11.1 (continued)

Marketing activity	What is success? The key performance indicator and its metric	Measurement mechanism	Cost of activity and measure	Value for money Achieved	Mechanism works	Future use of activity/ mechanism
Call centre	Perform to contract	Checks	OK	Yes	Yes	No change
Fulfilment – outsourced	Perform to contract	Checks	OK	Yes	Yes	OK
Telemarketing	Perform to contract	Checks	OK	Yes	Yes	Good value
Market reearch – outsourced	Perform to contract	Checks	OK	Yes	Yes	OK
Main research – in-house	Attitudes / awareness found or trend recorded Satisfactory measurement when used as a mechanism	Produce answers – information for decision taking	OK	Yes	Yes	Good briefing essential
Outsource contracts	To time and cost, within budget. Meet the brief	Observation. Accountant's figures	OK	Yes		
New product development	Attitudes / awareness found or trend recorded	Produce answers – information for decision taking	Under-funded	OK within limit set	Yes	Need more of it
Relaunch produce questionnaire	To same time as relaunch. Ideal response to be at 200 per week. Useful comments resulting	Observation. Record response quantity and quality. Comments found to be positively useful	OK	Yes – un-believable	Yes	Do this for all products
Corporate branding review (complete two months before main exhibition)	Satisfactory completion mid-year. Allows rectification at main exhibition possibility	Receive report and recommendations by mid-year	Slipped	Board aware		
Brand policing	No transgressions reported	Observation	?	No	No	Need a better mechanism

Part 4

Learn from experience

12

Pitfalls

There are certain inescapable business practices that apply to marketing activities, particularly promotional marketing activities, particularly in advertising. You should try, in all business dealings, using any supplier, to make sure they too can earn an honest buck. If you try to squeeze people too hard they will only reciprocate and often quite ingeniously win back money that they believe you fairly owe them. Some do go further and forget to reimburse you – the message is, be wary. You will also be pressurized into doing things just because it is the practice. Resist. Be different. That is what creative marketing is about. But don't be taken for a ride.

FACTS OF LIFE

Advertising

It is a truism that the risk element is less if the budget is small.

If you are a major brand then you will be under great pressure to match competitors' advertising. The production of commercials that are not different is probably a waste of money – no value-for-money marketing here. A difference is essential. But who is to challenge them? Not any supplier – too many vested interests. Only a person seeking value-for-money marketing.

Washing powder and car wars

The two major washing powder companies have routinely vied with each other for extra market share by spending enormous amounts on television advertising only to see the rival take the market share back when they splurge on advertising. The winners are neither of the companies advertising.

Car manufacturers equally spend large sums on their brands, both on television and in print. There are differences but do they really alter buying habits? Is this value-for-money marketing?

The media side will say that it is impossible to measure anything. A person seeking value-for-money marketing would insist on it.

The creative side can produce advertisements that are so smooth that they do not work; a rough edge is better – it is remembered. The same applies to service provision.

Service provision – perfection should not be an aspiration

The service element should consider offering a warmth and element of human error that makes it more attractive than perfection. This is particularly true when the service relates to a distress-related purchase such as a solicitor's practice.

The perfect office is not appreciated

A company supporting a national exhibition centre and the local area, providing a range of office services, was both inefficient and ineffective (as confirmed by client research). A major change in premises layout and working practices and investment in equipment produced both efficiency and effectiveness.

Subsequent client research found clients were unhappy with the perfection achieved. A number of parts of the service were then deliberately de-tuned to make customers feel that there was a human element and human frailty involved. Clients became really happy and routinely came back.

Sympathy in a solicitor's office

A solicitor is selling a distress-related purchase. The potential customer on the phone or walking into the office can encounter people prepared to fight to deny any access that disturbs a partner.

A Camberley solicitor's practice found a sympathetic receptionist brought in more business than any partner.

Advertising support for retail items

If your concept is to be sold through supermarkets, then assuming you want reasonable shelf space, you will be required to support your product with advertising. The advertising will probably need to be placed in the in-house magazine. The typical rate for a full-page colour advertisement in year 2000 was £13,000. The least that will be demanded by a retailer is a marketing plan.

TIPS

'Free' market research

Place a questionnaire inside your product. People will fill it in and send it to you. The response is enhanced if you invite them to enter a free prize draw. You will be amazed at the numbers that respond. Analyse the information for new product development and attitude and awareness purposes. Responses to questions about where customers purchase will indicate preferred distributors and areas of the country where your target market is strong.

Build a database of customers for customer panels, future direct mailings

Offer through a coupon – even printed onto the packaging – a product support leaflet (menus, methods of alternative use). People will volunteer information. You have names and addresses – ask them if they agree to you retaining them for further product information, joining future customer panels – then you can place their names and addresses on a database.

Chose your exhibition with care

Treat attendance figures with suspicion and the provenance of those attending previous exhibitions. Exhibitors will stretch figures in creative ways. Sometimes the actual visitor types are not those you have been led to expect. A sports show in the height of the summer held at a prestigious venue unsurprisingly attracted few of the sports professionals said by the exhibitors to be attending; the professionals were all out earning and they did not attend. The show was a flop for exhibitors.

Valuable customers

The customers that fully bond with your brand – that is they buy from nobody else – are your ideal customers. Tesco have achieved around 43 per cent bonding of their 100 high-value customers. Most firms are unaware of their valuable customers. It is often the case that a few customers generate most of the turnover. Some call this Pareto rule – that is 20 per cent of the customers provide 80 per cent of the business – as applicable across the board in all businesses. In the author's experience the percentage varies. In some businesses it is 5 per cent; sometimes it is much larger. What matters is that you should know and recognize the customer profile

---

Real-value customers of a financial services company

Analysis of the 500 or so customers of a financial services company found that only about 70 produced a reasonable income stream, of whom 18 were valuable and only 10 actually produced the majority of the turnover.

The profiles of the 10 customers were analysed and some 14,000 other potential customers were found that matched and a method of reaching them was tried and tested. A plan to attract 20 new customers of the preferred type each year was established. The non-producing customers were then sold to another financial services firm.

Who were the valuable clients in an accountant's firm?

Partners in a firm of accountants were asked to name their top 20 clients. This list was compared with the billings and the hours recorded. The top payer was not on the list.

Another client of the same firm was found to be receiving the benefit of some 10 times more hours than the billings charged.

A six-figure total sum of hours was found to have been lost in the transfer of 'hours' to billings through a processing error.

13

Scams

Trust is the key attribute. Some believe there has been an erosion of trust in the last decade. People assume that everyone must be fiddling. The position has not been helped by the erosion of the 15 per cent commission paid to agencies. Agency people are pragmatic; they will work to performance-related schemes, which is probably the best way.

There are three kinds of scams: fraud, which usually comes about through collusion, fiddling, and foolishness/incompetence.

A poor agency can rip off clients, underpay staff and close the business quickly. If an agency is screwed down too much it is likely to fiddle to increase its profitability.

When an agency is required to make major changes to copy by a client, for which the client does not want to pay, leaning on the supplier may work and the agency spreads the cost over the next five invoices. It has been known for an agency to seek out the printer and bribe him with whisky to stop a print run to allow changes to copy demanded by the client at the last moment.

ADVERTISING

Fraud

Fraud is only really effective if there is collusion.

Fiddling
If the agency deals with media owners, discounts can often include free airtime or space. The client does not know what the percentage is in time or space and can often end up paying for airtime or space that cost the agency nothing.

An agency will often raise justified positioning disputes over the placing of material in print and the dispute is resolved with a payback. An agency may do this as routine and not pass the dispute on to the client – or may fail to pass on the payback (unless the client is aware and complains).

Certification can be fallible. Circulation figures can be falsely raised – particularly for inserts, where the charge is per thousand inserts. Inserts may not be printed or dispersed as agreed. In one case only £7 million-worth of inserts were printed of an order for £10 million. Posters have been known to appear on poor sites under railway arches rather than the sites that the clients believed were being used. Posters are carefully placed along the chairman's route to work. Production can load a job plan.

Incompetence
An agency through incompetence may not challenge directors or photographers; unnecessary amounts of film may be shot. Creative buying can be sloppy.

Precautions
Cross-matching supplier invoices – back up invoices and carry out spot checks, although this does not avoid dodgy invoices.

It is possible to find out if you are paying over the odds – being overcharged – for airtime, by comparing network average against the station average.

A sensible precaution if you are spending £500,000 a year on advertising – that is £10,000 per week – is to employ a media audit person to confirm the spend is as agreed and that you are not being fiddled.

Similarly, an independent audit of production costs can be commissioned.

Challenging excesses every time is a basic start to finding out if you being taken for a ride.

SALES

The doubling mileages on claims has already been described under the section headed 'personal selling'.

One salesperson was always away on a call on a Wednesday – actually running another business. Working for others is a preoccupation with some salespersons.

Part 5

New business – control and measurement (including financial) for marketing activities

14

The key part marketing plays in start-ups

IS THERE A PROFITABLE MARKET FOR YOUR CONCEPT?

Business plans, many seeking around a million pounds of investment, are often submitted with a totally unsupported sales forecast. A one-row entry in a column of figures by months is put forward without justification as the expected sales figures. Marketing is a list of activities unrelated to any purpose. Yet the qualifications and experience of those putting forward the business plan are impressive.

If you have a new product or service to sell and you have an idea of a target market then you need answers to a number of fundamental questions, such as:

■ Is there a clearly accepted need by potential customers for your concept?
■ If not – perhaps because it is totally new – then potential customers will need to be educated and made aware of it. This will certainly take time and be expensive. Can your cash flow afford this?

▓ If there is an accepted need then what, if anything, is already being sold to satisfy that need? Why are people likely to purchase your concept rather than any direct or indirect competitive alternative?

▓ What is the total size of the market for your concept?

▓ How much of the total size can you realistically serve?

▓ If you are entering a new concept in an existing market you will need to overcome existing brands and any bonding between those brands and customers

▓ If you are entering a new concept in a new category you will have to overcome resistance to change – you will have to convey and have accepted the proposition that a new need exists and that your concept is the solution for that need. This again will take time and cost money.

▓ Do you have a clear understanding of how much time this may take?

▓ Can you make money out of the size you realistically can serve? Over what time? If everyone buys the concept – eventually? If only 50 per cent buy? If only 10 per cent buy?

▓ What are the channels of communication preferred by your potential customers?

▓ How is the need expressed by your potential customers?

▓ How do they view and describe your concept?

▓ Is the cost you propose likely to be valued highly by potential customers?

▓ If not, how are you to increase the value perception?

▓ Are there any price points favoured by your potential customers?

▓ Are your distribution and the time and manner in which your concept is to be sold acceptable to your potential customers?

▓ What buying processes do your potential customers follow to purchase similar concepts?

▓ Do the buying processes require proof of the 'six Cs'? How are you going to deliver the 'six Cs'?

▓ Is your concept likely to be an impulse purchase?

▓ Does the sales process you propose match the potential customer buying process?

▓ What customer relationships to bond to a brand are preferred by your potential customers?

▓ What consideration have you given to consistency in all the operation and marketing activities you propose?

Answers to the above questions will give a framework for the marketing activities you need to implement, starting with the potential customer at the point of sale. From this you can build backwards to all the activities that you need to have set in train before you make your first sale, let alone make sufficient money, while solving any cash-flow traps to make your business a success.

Clearly market research activity can assist. Desk research will provide some of the answers. You may well need to commission some primary research to find out answers or indeed carry out the market research yourself.

From the research you will be able to extract the answers to the 'six Cs' and provide the buying process that potential customers expect. This will highlight staff training needs. The concept packaging will need to be legal, comprehensive in terms of instruction, and attractive – you should have answers from the desk and primary research to help you with the design brief for the packaging. Put in a concept questionnaire.

Each of the market research marketing activities as their measurement of success should produce information to enable you to take a decision on how to proceed.

How and what marketing activity can reduce the risk of making no sales?

From the operational side will have come maximum output rates for your concept that you can both service and afford. You will have to set concept sales targets based on the cash flow and possible sales achievement.

Further information will have come from the market research commissioned to find answers to the questions raised above in 'Is there a profitable market for your concept?' You know the preferred channel of communication – the customer need and how it is expressed, the way they buy and the cost value they put on the concept; you also know how, where and when they want to buy it.

Market research to find the optimized launch footprint

Matching the potential customer area and media coverage area to potential sales targets and the maximum operational concept output rates will provide an optimized launch footprint. Where the area may be is suggested by the results of a market research market activity, commissioned by you, to find that answer.

You will then know where to launch, in what media, what to say and how to market and sell. You finally need to confirm your outlets and your distributors, train your staff and obtain stocks.

Promotional marketing activity

A mix of the marketing activities in Chapters 4 to 7 will be required. These need to concentrate on awareness and education in customer-tuned messages: messages that tell potential customers why your concept is the answer to their needs and why they can trust you to deliver.

As every promotional penny you spend is valuable, you measure every marketing activity and determine what works or does not work so that you only fund the marketing activities that bring results.

If unsure use a marketing consultant

If you are unsure of the marketing activities to employ then you need to use a marketing consultant to assist with the selection. This is particularly helpful if you are seeking a partner or funding in whatever form for your new business – potential backers are more likely to believe a third party.

15

Drawing together a marketing activities programme

EXAMPLE – A DOT.COM START-UP

By way of example, a draft business plan for a dot.com start-up is used here to show how to measure marketing. The example is based on a real proposal.

The start-up offers a concept – a mix of product and service – that is to be provided through the Internet. It is a personal service that is currently supplied by specialists, but this concept in future will allow individuals either to operate the personal service in whole by themselves or in part through further communication with a specialist via the Web site. It is accepted that there are charitable outlets in existence where some of the concept is provided at no cost now. The cost of the proposed concept anticipates a high margin. The cost is a mix of subscription for membership that buys the services and the purchase of products in support.

The operation presumes that potential customers will find the Web site and subscribe (some Web banners are planned as well as links to other specialists, affiliates and strategic partners' Web sites). Discounts on the concept will be used to encourage and motivate subscriptions. Subscribers will have access to password-protected areas on the Web site that will give further information and access to specialists.

The plan presumes that the potential customer will be happy with the name. The only non-Internet marketing activities planned are some advertising in magazines, the issuing of some press releases, and PR using radio and morning TV shows. Assuming that the Web site design is reasonable and the behind-the-scenes logistics and distribution are sufficient – what marketing activities should be undertaken to improve upon this plan?

The concept is only new in that delivery is via the Internet. There is already an established market for the concept and it is possible to get the concept free.

First marketing activity – market research

So what market research will be needed to determine what? A key question will be: is there a clearly accepted need by potential customers for the concept to be delivered by this medium – the Internet? A profile of these Internet-accepting potential customers can then be established. Is there any group within that profile, of innovative or early purchasers? These can help cash flow and provide references and early referrals.

How is the need expressed by these potential customers? How do they view and describe the concept?

The cost of the concept is set high; will this be acceptable to Internet-accepting potential customers? It can be obtained free now.

Do the potential customers favour any price points? Is the concept also an impulse purchase? This will decide whether the Web site has to just attract repeat visitors or whether it can accept single-purchase customers.

If the concept is not an impulse purchase, does the sales process proposed match the potential customer buying process? The Web site will certainly have to attract more visits if a buying process is followed.

The concept may be seen as impersonal delivery of a personal service – is that correct and still marketable?

When people consider the concept, are they persuaded to take it by themselves or are they likely to be persuaded more by family and friends? If the influence of family and friends is beneficial then interactive or direct-response TV might be more appropriate than the Internet.

Why are people likely to purchase the concept through the Internet rather than the existing outlets, especially when some can obtain the concept free? Clearly attitude and motivation are going to be key as to whether potential customers are likely to switch to the Internet, breaking existing concept provider bonds – this needs to be examined and the strength of bonds determined.

What customer relationships to bond to a brand are preferred by the potential customers?

This all provides strategic marketing input to the business plan.

Desk research may also be helpful. It leads to the realistic calculation of market size.

How many of the profiled potential customers are there? Is the cost proposed likely to be valued highly by potential customers? If not, how can an increase in the value perception be produced? Or will a lower cost be acceptable?

Can money be made out of the market size that realistically can be served and over what time? Would this only be the case if everyone buys the concept – eventually? If only 50 per cent buy? If only 10 per cent buy?

The sales targets can now be set and the number of subscribers set.

The business planning process

Business objectives and marketing objectives can now be drawn up:

■ To attract a target number of subscribers with the agreed profile to the Web site.
■ To achieve sales from each subscriber of a target number of concept purchases.
■ To create awareness of the Web site among the profile potential customers with a priority on innovators.
■ To raise the value perception of the concept.

Marketing activities

Promotional marketing activities that arise from the marketing objectives

The profile will help establish the advertising magazines to use. The way the need is expressed and the way the concept is described will assist copy preparation.

There may be a need to raise the value perception to achieve the cost – the price point preferred by potential customers.

Consideration should be given to consistency in all the operation and marketing activities proposed.

Measuring marketing activity

The marketing activities need to be measured. In a new business, early indication of success is required for any marketing activity to see that it is value-for-money marketing.

From the early indication you will be able to continue, increase, decrease or stop the marketing activity.

Each marketing activity should be split into two, a test and then the full activity. Measure the success of the test before full commitment. This means you will need to require every supplier to agree to a test first. Chapters 3 to 7 indicate ways of achieving small runs of literature or brochures. Test advertisements on sample audiences – use your own employees, families and friends. Test a Web site.

For marketing activities for awareness or education you will need a market research sample to confirm knowledge – or an attitude change. Act on the results. This will save wasted resources.

Look at the process of setting the criteria for success and the marketing mechanisms used in Chapters 8 to 11. The ring-fencing, budget setting and allocation of responsibility apply equally to a new business and an existing business.

16

Where start-ups should not skimp

Do not skimp on market research because you need sufficient desk research to demonstrate you can make money out of sales of your concept (sales are not determined by how much concept you can supply but 'how much the customer is prepared to buy'). Similarly, do not skimp on primary research to find out about the potential customers for your concept and to determine the messages to use and to match the preferred buying process.

For a new business – after market research marketing activity – promotional marketing activity is likely to be the major part of start-up.

Promotional marketing activity, however, is considered after you know that you have an opportunity to succeed. This means that it is vulnerable because. Cash flow is critical, so it is the most likely activity to be cut.

If you have no option but to cut promotional marketing activity, then *establish the core promotional marketing activities*. You should assess the benefits that accrue from carrying out each one.

Cut out the froth. It is easy to be attracted by a high-profile launch (with high costs) and the dream of instant universal fame, but the reality may be that it does not quite come off as you hoped and the result is a damp squib. If it is high risk then it is better to cut the activity and go for that which gives an assured return.

Keep the quality, reduce the time or size or colour. If you are planning commercials or advertisements then consider 10-second rather than 30-second commercials. Use quarter page rather than full page. Does your message work just as well in black and white rather than colour?

Reduce the scope – but keep the mix. If you need a particular combination of marketing activities, but it still costs too much, cut down the launch scope. Choose a potential customer-rich 'territory' first, where potential customers are likely to be more favourably tuned to your concept – and 'territory' that is rich with communication channels appropriate to your potential customer. It is better not to spread resources too thin – limit your area for launch to that of regional TV channel coverage, regional magazine coverage, local radio templates.

Do not skimp on advertising, PR and direct mail, sufficient for your target market:

■ to be aware of the concept – its benefits and features;
■ to educate the customer that it meets their needs;
■ to overcome the lack of imagination;
■ to overcome resistance to change.

Do not skimp on measurement – split marketing activities into two. Test and measure before the full marketing activity is implemented and measured. Then measure the main activity.

When cash is tight you need to know the value each marketing activity is contributing. That it is of value itself. Measurement is even easier to cut but it provides an early indication of value-for-money marketing.

NEW BUSINESS SUMMARY

In summary a new business marketing activity needs market research to establish the potential target market and its profile. This will:

■ describe the size and shape of the target market;
■ define what will need to be done in terms of the 'six Cs' to capture market share;

- confirm you can make money out of your venture;
- match your launch to your cash-flow capability;
- indicate the promotional marketing activities needed to assist the launch;
- confirm through early measurement of the marketing activity that you are choosing the marketing activities that give you value for money.

The new business needs promotional marketing to:

- create awareness;
- educate;
- improve or support value perception;
- grow and develop the brand;
- state the concept distribution (where potential customers can see and buy);
- start and build customer relationships.

Part 6

Advanced marketing measurement and tools

Professor Robert Shaw is one of the first to consider and advocate the importance of marketing measurement. This section is extracted, with his permission, from his book *Improving Marketing Effectiveness*, published by The Economist Books. Professor Shaw notes that, although management accounting has been around for a long time, there is no comparable discipline in marketing. The basic principles are widely accepted but practice lags behind theory.

All that is required is to measure inputs and measure outputs and then compare the results. However, presently it is as if a black box existed. In his book he invites us to explore that black box a little more.

Professor Shaw quotes Robert McNamara, the former head of the World Bank, as saying:

The first step is to measure whatever can be easily measured. That is okay as far as it goes.

The second step is to disregard that which can't be easily measured or to give it an arbitrary quantitative value. This is artificial and misleading.

The third step is to presume that what can't be measured easily isn't important. This is blindness.

The fourth step is to say that what can't be easily measured really doesn't exist. This is suicide.

17

Advanced marketing measurement

Professor Shaw found that there is much customer satisfaction research. Here it is recognized that the actual results as a snapshot are not useful; it is the trends that matter. BT used multiple regression analysis to compare three campaigns over the period 1986 to 1995. BT spent a total of £56 million on the campaigns, but they had a £294 million positive revenue impact. Interestingly it was the 'Its good to talk' that did the best, triggering an urge to use the telephone. BT found an amazing 217 per cent increase in calls made by women who said 'the advertising reminded me to call someone and I rang them'.

Professor Shaw developed in 1997 a Measurement System Assessment Tool (MSAT) Framework, which was taken from the most widely used tools from 130 companies surveyed. Despite the Bain finding that securing a repeat purchase gives much greater increase in profit – greater than 50 per cent – few are concerned with measuring this or the reverse, that is the reasons for contract cancellation. An existing customer is likely to buy more, give referrals and buy through cross-selling. Table 17.2 shows the definitions used in the marketing measurement MSAT tools, which is useful as an explanation of the advanced techniques available. The tools are in Chapter 18.

Professor Shaw finds:

- Over 50 per cent of people prefer to use new marketing measurement tools than tried and tested techniques.
- Only 25 per cent were satisfied with their marketing measurement tools.
- Only half track market share.
- Few track customer complaints.
- One-third track price premium.
- Distribution is tracked by 11 per cent.
- Traditional costing commonly distorts the allocation of costs.
- Many product extensions are unprofitable because of traditional costing methods.
- Companies collect data that are easy to collect rather than data that are useful or accurate.
- Speed is given higher priority than accuracy or relevance.
- Training in marketing measurement techniques is rare.
- Good interviewing, although a skilled activity, is not recognized widely as such.
- Marketing measurement is a topic charged with political implications and corporate infighting.

Professor Shaw's book explores a number of measurement methodologies. He also tables the four steps in development of marketing knowledge used by KMAT TM of which Table 17.1 is the extract for 'measurement'.

Table 17.1

Knowledge factor	Step 1. Cost and product driven	Step 2. Customer tool proliferation	Step 3. Co-ordinated customer metrics	Step 4. Integrated customer knowledge
Measurement	Mostly cost and management accounting; hard to analyse for marketing purposes	Tool proliferation; quality, needs, loyalty, satisfaction all measured in different ways	Rationalization and standardization of marketing tools	Dissemination of measurement; used to grow organizational knowledge

Table 17.2 *Definitions used in the Measurement System Assessment Tool (MSAT) framework*

Consumer measures

Attitudes, interests and opinions tracking	Market research studies that categorize consumers into segments on the basis of attitudes, interests and opinions and track the segment trends.
Complaints tracking	Recording of cosumer complaints, tracking them until resolved, and analysing the causes and resolutions of complaints.
Customer profitability tracking	Tracking the profits that an individual customer generates. To calculate it requires the allocation of costs to the customer. This usually depends on the use of activity-based costing.
Customer satisfaction tracking	Tracking of customer satisfaction with the product or service and its features.
Dissatisfaction tracking	Tracking of dissatisfaction and eliciting customers on reasons for dissatisfaction.
Lost or dormant customer analysis	Recording of lost or dormant customers and analysis of the reasons for their loss or inactivity.
Loyalty reward programme	Recording of customer loyalty levels and rewarding of loyal behaviour.
Market share trading	Tracking of brand sales in a category and total category sales, and plotting trends into the ratio.
Needs and wants segmentation	Market research studies that categorize consumers into segments on the basis of perceived needs and wants and track the segment trends.
New product adoption/diffusion trackiing	Identification of early adopters and late adopters and tracking of their behaviour as the new product enters the market.
Perceived quality/value tracking	Market research to identify customer perceptions of product quality or value or both and tracking changes over time.
Perceived service tracking	Market research to identify customer perceptions of service and tracking changes over time.
Perceptual mapping (positioning)	A graphic representation of the positions of brands within a market based on consumer perceptions gathered through market research.
Promotion/advertising effectiveness tracking	Tracking of advertising and promotion effects expressed in terms of return on investment of the advertising and promotion expenditure or other measures of effectiveness.
Repeat purchase/retention tracking	Tracking of repeat purchases from individual customers. In the case of infrequent purchases, this is represented as customer retention, or attrition.

Trade measures

Attitudes, interests and opinion rating	Market research studies which categorize trade customers into segments on the basis of attitudes, interests and opinions and track the segment trends.

Table 17.2 *(continued)*

Channel/trade profitability reporting	Tracking of the profits that an individual channel or trade customer generates.
Channel/trade customer satisfaction tracking	Tracking of customer satisfaction with the product or service and its features.
Distribution: availability, share of shelf, pipeline	Tracking of the product distribution in the supply chain, including availability, share of shelf, etc. Usually analysed down to individual store unit.
Efficient customer response	Organization of the supply chain, by sharing information between the supplier and trade customer in order to improve efficiency. This often involves electronic data interchange (EDI) and other computer methods.
Win/loss analysis	Tracking of new accounts won or bids lost along with reasons given by the customer.

General tools

Activity-based costing (ABC)	A system that accumulates costs for each of the activities of an organization and then assigns these costs to the products, services, or other items that caused the activity. ABC methods take into account the actual activities, cost drivers and processes required to generate products or services. Traditional methods of cost allocation typically rely on volume-based allocation using labour or machine hours.
Balanced scorecard	A performance measurement system that strikes a balance between financial and operating measures, links performance to regards and explicitly recognizes the diversity of stakeholders.
Brand equity financial evaluation	The goodwill that exists in the market towards a brand. A financial estimate of this value may sometimes be included on the balance sheet.
Competitive benchmarking	Comparing performance to the best achieved by competitors. Comparisons are made on the basis of performance ratios and unit costs.
Employee attitudes, interests and opinions	Market research studies that categorize employees into segments on the basis of attitudes, interests and opinions. Tracking of segment trends.
New product/brand portfolios strategy models	A system of grading new products and brands by reference to market share, market growth or similar variables. Used in planning. Methods include the BCG matrix.
Quality (actual) tracking	Technical measurement of quality against conformance standards. Widely used in total quality management.
Relative price tracking	Tracking of prices relative to those of competitors. Usually analysed by outlet (for example, retailer).
Service (actual) tracking	Technical measurement of service against conformance standards. Widely used in total quality management.

18

Advanced marketing measurement tools

Professor Shaw describes 20 marketing measurement tools in Part 3 of his book, to which reference should be made for detailed explanation and description. Only a summary is given here. (A definition of some of the terms used is given in Table 18.1.)

Professor Shaw prefaces the section with a number of cautions to avoid wasting resources. In order to make intelligent decisions about which measurement tools to use, it is important to understand the company perspective, its problems and priorities.

Marketing measurement tools must not be used slavishly and forever – like any marketing activity their usefulness has to be relevant, appropriate and timely. A growing business will need more tools. The need for a marketing measurement tool may be discarded in a declining environment. Expensive environmental scanning may only be important to undertake as new legislation is introduced.

There is no need to measure something if it is already freely available or can be obtained more cheaply or easily. The measurement activity must not be counterproductive or dominate. The information generated ought to be accepted by everyone. Lack of commitment can cause problems that may harm or undermine the case for measurement – all activities require some debugging – and resilience is often required to introduce new marketing measurement tools.

Table 18.1 *Advanced marketing measurement tools*

Marketing measuring tool	What is it?	What can result?	Why is it useful?	Who should use it?
Category health	Comparison of customer perceptions and values of a concept and the way that meets a specific customer need	A favourable or otherwise comparison of competitors in a category	It helps strategists who want to know the category to invest in	Large organizations
Category	Scorecard of indicators of future category health	You may be the best in your category but if your category is fading then your company is likely to decline	It helps strategists who want to know the category to invest in	Large organizations
Competitive threats	Scorecard of indicators that examines whether competition in a category is likely to change	Realization of a competitive threat from a new entrant offering a new type of concept	Examines competition coming in from a tangent – not main competitors	Banks, financial services, FMCG, large organizations
Market leadership	Scorecard of one or more of relative market share, purchase penetration or relative ownership penetration	The relative ranking of market share is found Brands that lead a category have a marketing advantage	Tracks competitive strength, drives management's expectation of profitability	Large organizations
Distribution leadership	An indicator based on distribution coverage, range, in-stock maintenance, display quality	The relative ranking of your brand especially where consumer preference is weak	Influence beneficially retailers, merchandising and range management	Key account managers
Price premium	Measure price of basket of goods and services. Affected by channel/basket's composition and weighting	A justification for maintaining a price premium, but with the wrong basket can give a misleading view	Tracks added value. The willingness of consumers to pay more for your concept than competitors	Large organizations

Brand valuation	FRS10 allows acquired brands to be capitalized on the balance sheet. It is an intangible asset	Increased asset value – shows building shareholder value	The new valuation, nothing hidden, allows more borrowing – may avoid under-priced, predatory approaches	All
Repeat purchase	Likelihood of customers repurchasing your brand versus that of competition	Patterns of 100% loyals, first brand loyalty, share of category shows up versus those that switch brands	Tangible evidence of loyalty, brand value, quality, satisfaction	All
Trial purchase	Behaviour of first-time buyers	Analysis of a new category or a new brand set in an existing category	Rapid penetration of a category is essential to long-term success and this gives early indication	Those launching a new brand in an existing category
Complaints	Measure numbers per period, sources of complaint, reasons and priority	Indication of poor quality in some part of concept. Used by customers as an alternative to exit	Well-handled complaints increase repeat purchase. Tip of iceberg as only one in 10 dissatisfied complain	All
Awareness	Identification of brand in sufficient detail to influence purchase. How well brand is associated with need	Better understanding of buying sequence and importance of content when purchase is made	Measures removal of barriers to purchase rather than just recall or recognition of brand	All
Satisfaction	Customer attainment of goals through concept purchase and consumption for existing buyers	Better understanding of buying sequence and importance of content when purchase is made	Evidences manufacturing, distribution and service meet customer expectation	
Customer involvement	Measurement of arousal associated with a purchase. At the bottom is habit; at the top personal interest	A bias where the minority view dominates the mass view leading to misjudging the market	High involvement can lead to referral and recommendations to purchase	

Table 18.1 (continued)

Marketing measuring tool	What is it?	What can result?	Why is it useful?	Who should use it?
Brand image endorsement	Scorecoard of measures that show customer brand preference	A measure of organization and brand image endorsement is obtained. Tracks brand health over time	Defines the customer view of what is relevant, credible and distinctive to the brand, allowing extensions	All
Channel franchise	Measurement of trade and distributor attitude to suppliers	Discovery and diagnosis of problems with distribution leadership	If preferred supplier status is achieved it can reduce costs of doing business, improved display, stock levels	Organizations that have channels
Quality	Many different measure with customer perceived quality beginning to dominate	Discovery of problems, improvements in manufacturing, distribution, service	Signals concept's value positioning. Advertising can be used to achieve a high level of quality before experience	For all new concept launches
Corporate marketing support	Measures how much support is given to brands and to the marketing mix. Many models exist	Relates budgets to marketing activities. Can highlight marketing waste	As a yardstick for assessing the correct amount of resource is being allocated to marketing	Strategic interest or for investors
Marketing mix productivity	Compares mix elements	Finds best mix of mix	Gives rate per head, per day	FMCG, catalogue companies
Innovation benchmarks	Measures degree and speed of innovation and in competitors	Better long-term performance	Helps a company survive	Short concept life cycle firms
Marketing waste	Unneeded or cancelled marketing spend – measures waste	Saves money	Removes spending binges which try to spend to budget to avoid being cut next period	All

Marketing measurement tools are not a quick fix – many are carrying out tracking activity as their title proclaims.

Figure 18.1 published by *Marketing Business* in April 2001 produces a useful summary of Professor Shaw's thinking on how measurement specifying fits into the marketing decision-making cycle.

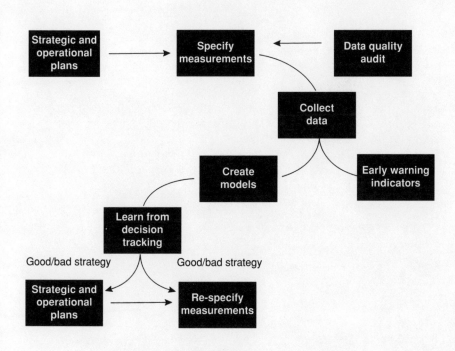

Figure 18.1 *Marketing decision-making cycle*

Part 7

How well did you do?

This part tries to put the end result of the process into perspective to see whether you have obtained value from it. It also looks at your team to see how well they did. To conclude, there is a summary chapter at the end of this section – the contents of this book in a Nutshell.

19

Performance evaluation

HOW WELL ARE YOU DOING THIS YEAR OR HOW WELL DID YOU DO LAST YEAR?

As an exercise, you may wish to carry out the self-assessment on your business this year (or last year if you can recall all that happened that far back).

A self-assessment form is provided as Table 19.1.

You should enter your business objectives above the table – are they SMART? Then enter marketing objectives that follow from the business objectives (or the ones that you used).

If you are carrying out this self-assessment you now adopt the role of the person responsible for the marketing activity. You and/or your team enter marketing activities that achieve the marketing objectives (or the marketing activities that you used) in the table in the first column.

You will need to apportion the tasks so that every marketing activity is someone's responsibility.

Now enter your team's assessment of how success will be judged (or if you are assessing last year what you used then) – these are the key performance indicators.

Then decide how are you going to measure that achievement – what mechanism will you use?

Has that thought process and filling in the table led you to ques-

Table 19.1 *Self-assessment – last year or this year*

Business objectives: 1.   2.   3.
                    4.   5.   6.

Are the business objectives SMART? (S = Specific, M = Measurable, A = Agreed, R = Reasonable, T = Timebound)

Marketing activity	What is success? Key performance indicator and its metric	Measurement mechanism	Cost of activity and measurement	Value for money achieved	Mechanism works	Future use of activity/ mechanism
Marketing objectives						
Marketing activities						

tion why you are undertaking any marketing activity? Has it caused you to tighten up your marketing objectives? If yes, then this process has already proved worthwhile.

Finally cost the marketing activities and the measurement mechanism. You now have a budget. If the budget cost is too large you will need to prune until it reaches a figure with which you are happy. You now have a marketing plan.

The appraisal process will set work objectives for people based on the marketing activities for which they are responsible.

The revised and agreed plan is then implemented.

As each marketing activity is completed you can record whether it has indeed been a success based on the measure of success you set and the cost: is it value-for-money marketing? If yes, then you have benefited by the process that this book advocates.

Fill in the table and then analyse the results as a whole – learn lessons for the next business planning process.

Carry out appraisals.

Even if you do not achieve value-for-money marketing across the board first time around, at least you will know why and you will have remedied the errors before next time. More benefit will come as you repeat and refine the process and as you achieve more value-for-money marketing.

20

Performance assessment and bonuses

MEASURING PEOPLE PERFORMANCE

The Investor in People appraisal system is recommended throughout this book. A job description specifies the person that is suited to fill that post and the activities that the post holder is likely to undertake. An appraisal form is a collection of work objectives – about seven work objectives are usually set. Each work objective sets a target of achievement for an individual for the next reporting period.

A work objective must be SMART (S = Specific, M = Measurable, A = Agreed, R = Reasonable, T = Timebound).

Work objectives are agreed by both the appraiser and appraised. The appraiser is usually the line manager. A reporting period is usually one year.

Interim reviews may be carried out during the year. These allow agreed changes to the work objectives in the light of experience and changing circumstances. They also allow a glimpse of progress towards the attainment of the work objectives.

At the end of the year the appraised carry out a self-assessment of their performance against the work objectives. The appraiser does the same. Each work objective is agreed as 'met', 'nearly met' or 'not met'.

A right of appeal is available to a person more senior than the line manager. Work objectives are then set for the next period.

Typically firms use the results of the appraisals to decide promotions, salary rises, and the line of succession planning.

CARRYING OUT THE APPRAISALS ON YOUR MARKETING STAFF

At the point in the business planning process where marketing activities were agreed you decided single responsibility for the marketing activities to make sure responsibility for the marketing activity was clear. The person responsible for the marketing activity was asked to state what would be 'success' for that marketing activity. The measuring mechanism was agreed soon after. The work objectives based on the marketing activities were also agreed at an appraisal interview.

At the end of the year each marketing activity is assessed in terms of whether it is 'value for money'. The appraisal held after can then take account of the person and how they handled the marketing activity for which they were responsible and the work objective that relates to it.

For example, the Web site person in Chapters 8 to 11 would have 'not met' their work objective relating to the Web site. The fault may be that they chose a poor measure for success or an unsuitable measurement mechanism. Clearly they were not up to the task on either count. It is more likely that they actually were not able to deliver a Web site to meet the need. In mitigation, if they were instructed to produce the Web site in a certain way and protested at the time that it would not work then that would make them less culpable. The manager would also have a responsibility here. The person responsible for the high-profile event would have met their work objective and would be considered favourably.

REWARDING YOUR STAFF

As suggested above – promotions, salary increases, line of succession planning might follow from appraisals. Equally, those who have not met work objectives would expect either further remedial training or demotion, salary reduction and no prospects. In the extreme they would be removed from their posts.

BONUS OF A 'MEASURE-ALL-MARKETING-ACTIVITIES' CULTURE

If people are rewarded through the results of the appraisal scheme, which takes account of work objectives set regarding their responsibility for marketing activities, a keen interest will be established subsequently in the selection of marketing activities, the definition of successful achievement and the measuring mechanism. People are less likely to select marketing activities that are unlikely to give value for money, in their own interest. They may tend to give a conservative success criterion but this may work against them as they will observe.

A natural balance will eventually be reached. As the cost of the measuring mechanism is included in the marketing activity, an optimized measuring mechanism will also surface. The extra cost of measuring will soon be overtaken by the reduction of wasted marketing resources and below-par performance from those responsible for marketing activities.

21

In a nutshell - summary of the book

To find again any part of the book please refer to the contents list at the front of the book or use the Index.

THIS BOOK'S PURPOSE

Chapter 1

The preface states this book has one purpose:

> To persuade you of the benefits of measuring each and every marketing activity such that you actually implement this proposal, at a stroke. And in your business, so you can find out whether you are getting value for money from marketing.

The introduction at Chapter 1 and essential information in appendices, top and tail the book.

The solution offered in the first chapter of this book, if you are persuaded to accept the purpose, is twofold:

> First, the simple but bold expedient of persuading you to state that 'in your organization - your business - all marketing activities are to be measured in future' and Second, offering you for your use, or use by those responsible for marketing activity, the measurement mechanisms needed.

THE MARKETING PROCESS

Chapter 2

This chapter describes, to ensure the same start point for readers:

1 the business process – how a business audit leads to drawing up SMART business objectives which, in turn, lead to a plan – in whatever format. Business objectives logically lead to marketing objectives.
2 the customer viewpoint:
   - the effect of branding on a customer – from consistency comes confidence and ultimately bonding;
   - the need for the sales process to match the customer's buying process;
   - the customer view – the 6Cs – which is how a customer analyses the benefits and features that sell the product.
3 the marketing activities which support:
   - the business process – helping strategic decision taking;
   - the business operation – helping achieve marketing and hence business objectives.

MARKETING ACTIVITIES AND THEIR MEASUREMENT

Part 2

Description of marketing activities and the measurement mechanisms for them are covered in Part 2.

Chapter 3 covers the mechanisms available to measure non-promotional marketing activities such as:

■ staff performance;
■ contract staff performance (contract performance is covered in chapter 4);
■ overhead's support;
■ and the non-promotional elements that make up the 6Cs:
   - concept – the product service itself and new concept development;
   - cost – the value perception to the customer;

- convenience – the behind scenes activities of ease-of-purchase, logistics, stock levels, distribution.

Chapters 4 to 7 cover promotional marketing activities – their description, use and measurement, under four headings:

- ■ new media;
- ■ direct marketing communication;
- ■ one-on-one communication;
- ■ general communications.

APPLICTION TO AN EXISTING BUSINESS

Part 3

Chapters 8 to 11 give an example where the process of applying measuring mechanisms to all marketing activity is illustrated for an existing business. The example takes the process through:

- ■ setting of business objectives, where marketing activities help with strategic decision making; success of those marketing activities rated by the quality of the information resulting as being sufficient to take the decision for which the market activity was implemented, measured by the decision makers and from which marketing objectives result.
- ■ deciding the measurement mechanisms for the marketing objectives themselves.
- ■ determining the promotional marketing activities needed to fulfil the marketing objectives, the definition of successful achievement for success and the mechanisms for measurement of each marketing activity and the contribution made towards the marketing objective.
- ■ the deployment of non-promotional marketing activities in support of the business operation.
- ■ an assessment of likely outcomes of the measuring of marketing activities demonstrating the success or otherwise and suggestions for action.
- ■ the whole process of spending it, measuring it and achieving value, shows 'value for money marketing' works.

PITFALLS

Part 4

Chapters 12 and 13 cover pitfalls – the facts of life about marketing, tips and scams.

APPLICATION TO A START-UP

Part 5

Chapters 14 to 16 give an example where the process of applying measuring mechanisms to each marketing activity is illustrated for a new business. The example takes the process through what new business marketing activity needs:

■ market research to establish the size and shape of the potential target market and its profile, this will:
  – describe the size and shape of the target market;
  – define what will need to be done in terms of the 6Cs to capture market share;
  – confirm you can make money out of your venture;
  – match your launch to your cash flow capability.
■ promotional marketing activities needed to assist the launch;
■ confirmation, through an early measurement test of the marketing activity.

ADVANCED MEASUREMENT

Part 6

Chapters 17 and 18 look at advanced marketing activity measurement mechanisms, a precis provided by Professor Robert Shaw.

HOW WELL DID YOU DO?

Part 7

Chapters 19 and 20 includes a self assessment form and how you appraise the performance of your staff.
   Chapter 21 is a summary of the other chapters – given here!

Appendix 1 is a request for feedback so the author and publisher can measure their achievement. Have we given you value for money?

Appendix 2 lists Reference Material

Finally there is an index.

Appendix 1: Measuring the effectiveness of this book

The author and the publisher, Kogan Page, would welcome feedback on this book. Feedback may take any number of forms – please write or e-mail (roddywpmullin@hotmail.com) or visit the Kogan Page Web site (www.kogan-page.com). Please also answer our 11 questions given below.

The key piece of information that we would like to know from you is whether we have met this book's purpose. Have we persuaded you to accept that it is of benefit to measure each and every marketing activity and have you actually implemented this proposal at a stroke, in your business? Please write or e-mail and let us know whether:

1. You were persuaded by this book to measure marketing.
2. You did accept our challenge and now measure every marketing activity in your business.

We included in this book many measurement mechanisms to help you yourself measure marketing activity, or for use by those responsible to you for marketing activity.

3. Did you or those responsible to you find the measurement mechanisms suggested useful?
4. What was the most useful measurement mechanism and why?
5. Did you use any other mechanisms? Please give details.

Finally, we would like to find out whether:

6. You have enjoyed finding out that you can get value from marketing?
7. If you have a result, did you get value?
8. What was the most valuable marketing activity to measure?
9. What have you done as a result?

If you have a result and now know that some of your marketing has not been of value:

10. We would like to know which marketing activities were of least value?
11. Have you been the subject of a management failure or scam? Please give details.

You may have had a mix of results – some parts being of value other not. We would appreciate any additional general comments.

A free, sponsored demo CD on market research from Snap Survey Software of their SNAP software is given away with every copy.

Appendix 2: Reference material

BOOKS

General marketing books

A useful quick practical book on marketing is:

Davey, R and Jacks, A (2000) *How to be Better at Marketing*, Kogan Page, London

A valuable book that is also practical and gives inexpensive ideas for marketing:

Forsyth, P (2000) *Marketing on a Tight Budget*, Kogan Page, London

The written equivalent of a Web site's 'frequently asked questions':

Smith, P (1999) *Great Answers to Tough Marketing Questions*, Kogan Page, London

And for general creative help:

Yadin, D (1998) *Creative Marketing Communications*, Kogan Page, London

Measuring marketing books

The book of which Chapters 14 and 15 in this book are a précis:

Shaw, R (1998) *Improving Marketing Effectiveness*, The Economist Books, London

This book is mentioned in Chapter 1:

Ambler, T (2000) *Marketing and the Bottom Line*, Financial Times/Prentice Hall, London

As is this book:
Doyle, P (2000) *Value-Based Marketing*, Wiley, Chichester.

Direct marketing

For a lovely readable book see the fourth edition of

Bird, D (2000) *Commonsense Direct Marketing*, Kogan Page, London

As an essential guide for beginners covering direct mail, direct-response advertising, door-to-door, piggybacks, telemarketing, the Internet and catalogues:

Donovan, J (2000) *DIY Direct Marketing*, Kogan Page, London

Advertising

David, M (1997) *Successful Advertising*, Cassell, London

Market research

The best book the author has found on market research:

Bim, R (2000) *The Handbook of International Market Research*, Kogan Page, London

Competition

Fisher, J (2000) *How to Beat Your Competitors*, Kogan Page, London

Conferences

Fisher, J (2000) *How to Run a Successful Conference*, Kogan Page, London

Incentive schemes

Covering travel incentive vouchers, merchandise bonus, shares and smart cards designed to increase your staff motivation and performance:

Fisher, J (2000) *How to Run Successful Incentive Schemes*, Kogan Page, London

Agencies

A book covering advertising, sales, promotion, market research agencies, public relations, direct mail and marketing consultants, exhibition services – this book is full of useful contacts:

Smith, G (1994) *Getting the Best from Agencies*, Kogan Page, London

Useful firms

Extranets, intranets, the Internet
www.MarketingNet.com (also their book: Bickerton, P, Bickerton, M and Simpson-Holley (1998) *Cyberstrategy*, Butterworth-Heinemann, Oxford

Mobile Internet:
www.airmedia.co.uk
www.nightfly.co.uk
www.distractions.co.com – a site with a fantastic beat and a chance to play with a WAP phone.

Interactive TV
Open... +44 (0)20 7332 7000/(0)870 60 60 60 4 – the Web site is barred
www.grange-direct.co.uk – Jenny Moseley is the expert on MailSort and is the present DMA Chairman.

Web-based directories

Seek (0800 169 6820) (www.seekdirectory.co.uk)

Data protection Web sites

www.dataprotection.gov.uk/
www.ccta.gov.uk/dpr/dpdoc.nsf
www.dpr.gov.uk/
www.hmso.gov.uk/acts1998/19980029.htm
www.acs.ohio-state.edu/units/law/swire1/psecind.htm
www.truste.org/

The EU Distance Selling Regulations – see Institute of Sales Promotion Web site – www.isp.org.uk

Marketing training

The Chartered Institute of Marketing (CIM) runs many courses designed to train anybody from any discipline in the appropriate part of marketing for the task in hand. Telephone 0 (044) 1628 427200 for CIM training (www.cim.co.uk).

Index

Marketing in Action Series

Series editor: Daniel Yadin

Lively, yet 'easy to read', each book in this series is a clear, concise, action-oriented and up-to-date summary of a specific marketing topic. Each book avoids jargon and provides busy marketers with valuable, practical step-by-step guidance. Ideal for marketers in organizations of any size, the books will also appeal to students studying for formal qualifications in marketing (CAM, CIM).

Titles available are:

Branding (2nd edition)

Business Market Research

Creative Marketing Communications (2nd edition)

Customer Relationship Marketing (2nd edition)

Direct Marketing

The Effective Use of Sponsorship

Getting the Best from Agencies and Other Outside Services

A Guide to Web Marketing

How to Produce Successful Advertising (2nd edition)

Introduction to International Marketing

Introduction to Marketing

Marketing a Service for Profit

Marketing for the Voluntary Sector

A Practical Guide to Integrated Marketing Communications (revised edition)

Strategic Marketing, Planning and Evaluation

Successful Product Management (2nd edition)

Value for Money Marketing

Daniel Yadin is a consultant in marketing communications. A writer and author, and former Course Director at the Chartered Institute of Marketing, he lectures widely at educational and training organizations in Britain and overseas. He is co-author of books on public relations and advertising, and author of *Creative Marketing Communications* in this series.

Kogan Page Ltd
120 Pentonville Road
London N1 9JN
www.kogan-page.co.uk

The CD ROM supplied with this book was produced and supplied by Snap® Survey Software, Mercator Computer Systems Limited.

If you wish to obtain further information about Snap® Survey Software or have any queries regarding the CD ROM, please contact Snap Software at the following addresses:

Snap Software (Head Office)
Mercator Computer Systems Limited
5 Mead Court
Thornbury
Bristol BS35 3UW
Tel: (01454) 281211
Fax: (01454) 281216
www.surveyshop.com
e-mail: info@surveyshop.com

Snap Software (London Office)
Mercator Computer Systems Limited
Liberty House
222 Regent Street
London W1B 5TR
Tel: (020) 7297 2003
e-mail: sales@mercator.co.uk